"In *Gifts from Friends We Never Wanted*, Virginia Herbers invites us to reimagine whom we might think of as a friend (grief, betrayal, doubt, disappointment) and marvel at the gifts they offer (wonder, reverence, choice, perspective). Reflective, insightful, and sparkling with humor and warmth, the book opens us to moments in the Gospels and Herbers' own life when a gift was revealed through loss, lack, or even a grave mistake. In each of the ten stories, Herbers provides a wealth of historical context and close reading to defamiliarize the characters we think we know well, showing us the how the messy, confusing, and worrisome can actually lead to consolation. This book is a warm conversation with a wise friend who helps us notice in the Gospels, our own lives, and everyday challenges how much the gifts of love and grace abound."

— Melody S. Gee, author of *We Carry Smoke and Paper: Essays on the Grief and Hope of Conversion*

"In *Gifts from Friends We Never Wanted*, Virginia Herbers continues the creative look at Scripture and life that she began in her previous volume, *Gifts from Friends We've Yet to Meet*. But this time she goes deeper into the darkness of life's many mysteries, taking us along for the ride as she journeys into the many unwanted moments of life that still have the capacity to lead us into God's presence and providence. It's a journey worth taking."

— Steve Givens, spiritual director, author of *Embraced by God: Facing Chemotherapy with Faith*, and executive director of Bridges Foundation

"Virginia Herbers' latest work is the fruit of sustained reflection on ten different figures in the Scriptures. She unites sound exegetical analysis with imaginative contemplation of personalities like Mary, Joseph, Elizabeth, Andrew, and Peter, among others, always generating some fresh perspective and original insight into these individuals. Her readers will also come away with a new understanding of themselves, thanks to her perceptive observations."

— Very Rev. Seán Charles Martin, STD, president emeritus, Aquinas Institute of Theology

"In a world that continues to encourage us to be perfect, Virginia writes about the graces received through the times and seasons that we may want to ignore. Instead of wishing our struggles away, she invites us, through our heroes of Scripture, to consider how we are 'blessed in the mess' of our daily lives. Read this with hope: There is joy waiting in the wings!"

— Danielle Harrison, retreat director and principal, Mission Faith Equity Consulting

Gifts from Friends
We Never Wanted

Biblical Journeys of Grace

Virginia Herbers

LITURGICAL PRESS
Collegeville, Minnesota

litpress.org

Cover art courtesy of Getty Images.

Scripture texts in this work are taken from the *New American Bible, revised edition* © 2010, 1991, 1986, 1970 Confraternity of Christian Doctrine, Washington, DC and are used by permission of the copyright owner. All Rights Reserved. No part of the New American Bible may be reproduced in any form without permission in writing from the copyright owner.

Excerpts from the English translation of the *Catechism of the Catholic Church* for use in the United States of America copyright © 1994, United States Catholic Conference, Inc.—Libreria Editrice Vaticana. English translation of the *Catechism of the Catholic Church: Modifications from the Editio Typica* copyright © 1997, United States Catholic Conference, Inc.—Libreria Editrice Vaticana. Used with Permission.

© 2024 by Virginia Herbers
Published by Liturgical Press, Collegeville, Minnesota. All rights reserved. No part of this book may be used or reproduced in any manner whatsoever, except brief quotations in reviews, without written permission of Liturgical Press, Saint John's Abbey, PO Box 7500, Collegeville, MN 56321-7500. Printed in the United States of America.

1   2   3   4   5   6   7   8   9

Library of Congress Cataloging-in-Publication Data

Names: Herbers, Virginia, author.
Title: Gifts from friends we never wanted : biblical journeys of grace / Virginia Herbers.
Description: Collegeville, Minnesota : Liturgical Press, [2024] | Includes bibliographical references. | Summary: "Following the same pattern as her first book, Gifts from Friends We've Yet to Meet, Herbers chooses a gospel character to accompany us as we engage uninvited "friends," weaving together the stories of Jesus's contemporaries, his response to their foibles, and stories from her own experiences"—Provided by publisher.
Identifiers: LCCN 2024013064 (print) | LCCN 2024013065 (ebook) | ISBN 9798400800184 (trade paperback) | ISBN 9798400800191 (epub) | ISBN 9780814688922 (pdf)
Subjects: LCSH: Gifts—Religious aspects—Christianity. | Strangers—Religious aspects—Christianity. | BISAC: RELIGION / Biblical Meditations / New Testament | RELIGION / Biblical Studies / New Testament / Jesus, the Gospels & Acts
Classification: LCC BR115.G54 H48 2024 (print) | LCC BR115.G54 (ebook) | DDC 234—dc23/eng/20240522
LC record available at https://lccn.loc.gov/2024013064
LC ebook record available at https://lccn.loc.gov/2024013065

*In thanksgiving for all the friends I never wanted,
especially failure, regret, embarrassment, and humiliation.
I neither invited nor welcomed you,
but you have enriched me beyond measure.*

I am grateful.

Contents

Introduction 1

1 Elizabeth *Befriending Grief:*
The Gift of the Second-to-Last Page 5

2 Joseph *Befriending Incompletion:*
The Gift of Wonder 15

3 Andrew *Befriending Second Place:*
The Gift of Perspective 27

4 Martha *Befriending Worry: The Gift of Reverence* 39

5 John the Baptist
Befriending Doubt: The Gift of Choice 49

6 Judas *Befriending Betrayal:*
The Gift of the Whole Truth 59

7 Mary *Befriending Anguish: The Gift of Pondering* 73

8 Longinus *Befriending Error: The Gift of Conversion* 85

9 Cleopas *Befriending Disappointment:*
The Gift of Presence 99

10 Peter *Befriending Failure: The Gift of Authority* 109

Afterword 121

Acknowledgments 123

Bibliography 125

Introduction

I imagine the title of this work may evoke questions. After all, what kinds of friends would we not want? Well, that's easy—the kind we don't identify as friends at first glance: failure, isolation, sin, to name a few. When these folks and all their ugly relatives come visiting, we likely don't go running out to greet them with open arms. We do not readily identify them as friends.

But what if, upon closer inspection, we realize that they aren't actually enemies either? What if, in the hand of God, they become vehicles of grace and instruments of love? These undesirable elements of our own lives that demonstrate our weakness, error, and sinfulness (and notice, I am focusing on the unsavory memories of what *we've* done, not on what has been done *to* us)—what if these experiences we'd prefer to eliminate from our past, present, and future actually become transformed into blessings of unimaginable worth? Wouldn't we then name them gifts? And wouldn't we have to admit that even if they were at first repugnant, they have actually become friends—friends we never really wanted and certainly never went looking for, but whom now we can't imagine living without?

I recently spoke with some dear friends about a series of events in my own life that fill me with sadness, regret, embarrassment, and a touch of shame. Two of them immediately offered generous words of comfort and reassurance, but the third did not. Instead, he said, "You've used some really tough descriptors for yourself in this conversation. Maybe it's too soon, so forgive me if that's true, but have you considered the possibility that all those things you described—heartbreak, guilt, failure—might actually be a source of grace, the very vehicle through which God will show up for you?" I sat across from him, stunned, feeling as if he'd just thrown cold water in my face. This was a message I had often preached to others, a spiritual reality I believed with all my heart for everyone else. But I had never, *ever* considered it to be equally true for myself.

"No," I responded flatly.

Ever so gently, he ventured, "So . . . do you think it might be worth considering?"

I took another sip of my drink before muttering, "Maybe," but what I was really thinking was, "Gosh darn it, Rob. How dare you challenge me to put into practice what I profess to believe, asking me to apply faith principles to my own life!"

Truth be told, in that brief exchange Rob had articulated the heart of what this book gets at: *sometimes the deepest wounds of our lives need to be entered, not nursed.* Only then can those wounds become blessing and grace rather than just nasty scars that disfigure and hinder us.

I am not talking about "turning lemons into lemonade" or "just getting over it, for cryin' out loud." No, the topics in these next chapters are painful (sometimes embarrassing) realities, and we ought neither sugarcoat their sourness into something palatable nor bypass honest reflection in order to arrive at a happy ending.

When we have been petty or cowardly, we might instinctually try to justify or gloss over what happened, but if we do, we will miss the grace and invitation latent in the experience. When we have failed, betrayed someone, or collapsed in despair, we may recoil from the memory of the experience, but until we dare to face it straight on, we will never know healing. Just as Jacob had to wrestle all night long with the angel before he received a blessing (Genesis 32), so must we wrestle with the truth of our own imperfections until we can eke out the grace and beauty they have to offer.

St. Paul wrote to the Corinthians that he was given a "thorn in the flesh" to prevent him from becoming too self-inflated. This weakness of his was the source of such consternation (or humiliation?) that he begged God to remove it. God said no, "My grace is sufficient for you." Once Paul could accept that his weaknesses were the very portal through which God's power and perfection worked, he was able to befriend those weaknesses and even boast of them. (See 2 Corinthians 12, although I do find it necessary to add that for as much as Paul said he would rather "boast most gladly of [his] weaknesses," he never once actually told us what they were!)

We will regard each of the difficult experiences addressed in these next chapters as a "friend we never wanted," but a friend nonetheless. To encourage us in this very vulnerable space, someone from the gospels will accompany each reflection. Let's hope that these individuals, who knew Jesus Christ personally and whose imperfections were abundantly apparent to him, just might help us believe that our own flaws, when exposed to the light of true Love, can provide us with gifts beyond measure.

Chapter 1: Elizabeth

Befriending Grief:
The Gift of the Second-to-Last Page

The meeting of Zechariah and Elizabeth

In the days of Herod, King of Judea, there was a priest named Zechariah of the priestly division of Abijah; his wife was from the daughters of Aaron, and her name was Elizabeth. Both were righteous in the eyes of God, observing all the commandments and ordinances of the

Lord blamelessly. But they had no child, because Elizabeth was barren and both were advanced in years. Once when he was serving as priest in his division's turn before God, according to the practice of the priestly service, he was chosen by lot to enter the sanctuary of the Lord to burn incense. Then, when the whole assembly of the people was praying outside at the hour of the incense offering, the angel of the Lord appeared to him, standing at the right of the altar of incense.

Zechariah was troubled by what he saw, and fear came upon him. But the angel said to him, "Do not be afraid, Zechariah, because your prayer has been heard. Your wife Elizabeth will bear you a son, and you shall name him John. And you will have joy and gladness, and many will rejoice at his birth, for he will be great in the sight of [the] Lord."

Then Zechariah said to the angel, "How shall I know this? For I am an old man, and my wife is advanced in years." And the angel said to him in reply, "I am Gabriel, who stand before God. I was sent to speak to you and to announce to you this good news. But now you will be speechless and unable to talk until the day these things take place, because you did not believe my words, which will be fulfilled at their proper time."

Then, when his days of ministry were completed, he went home. After this time his wife Elizabeth conceived, and she went into seclusion for five months, saying, "So has the Lord done for me at a time when he has seen fit to take away my disgrace before others."

During those days Mary set out and traveled to the hill country in haste to a town of Judah, where she entered the house of Zechariah and greeted Elizabeth. When Elizabeth heard Mary's greeting, the infant leaped in her womb, and Elizabeth, filled with the holy Spirit, cried out in a loud voice and said, "Most blessed are you among women, and blessed is the fruit of your womb. And how does this happen to me, that the mother of my Lord should come to me?

For at the moment the sound of your greeting reached my ears, the infant in my womb leaped for joy. Blessed are you who believed that what was spoken to you by the Lord would be fulfilled."

Mary remained with her about three months and then returned to her home.

When the time arrived for Elizabeth to have her child she gave birth to a son. Her neighbors and relatives heard that the Lord had shown his great mercy toward her, and they rejoiced with her. When they came on the eighth day to circumcise the child, they were going to call him Zechariah after his father, but his mother said in reply, "No. He will be called John." But they answered her, "There is no one among your relatives who has this name." So they made signs, asking his father what he wished him to be called. He asked for a tablet and wrote, "John is his name," and all were amazed. Immediately his mouth was opened, his tongue freed, and he spoke blessing God.

—Luke 1:5-15, 18-20, 23-25, 39-45, 56-64

Yeah, it's a long passage, but before you decide to skip the gospel excerpt above and just read this chapter, answer me this: how much time or thought have you ever given to Elizabeth? Before quite recently, my own answer to this was "very little," so if yours is similar, go back and read the excerpt in full.

Now: Elizabeth. All that we know of her is in reference to someone else: she is descendant of Aaron, wife of Zechariah, mother of John the Baptist, cousin of Mary. And throughout most of her life, into her "advanced years," she was without child. Beyond the heartache this must have been for her and her husband, it was also a public humiliation among her community. The social reproach that resulted from being childless in Jewish culture had religious roots, reaching deep into the Genesis histories of Sarai, Rebekah, Rachel and Hannah.[1] A woman's inability to provide a child—particularly a son—was perceived as a failure of the worst kind, despite the fact that both Elizabeth and Zechariah "were righteous in the eyes of God, observing blamelessly all the commandments and ordinances of the Lord." Elizabeth spent a lifetime in prayer, trust, hope, and devotion, yet in her old age she ultimately had to accept the heartbreak of barrenness.

I learned long ago that we don't get what we deserve in life—and although that's not necessarily a completely negative reality, it is not always easy to accept either. Good things don't only happen to good people, or bad things only to bad people. In reality, all kinds of things happen to all kinds of people. But when it comes to a person like Elizabeth, her lifelong sadness is a little hard to take. I've known a few Elizabeths in my life—folks who are good to the core, golden-hearted, and who seem to experience more than their fair share of tragedy, pain, or loss. Although the question of "why does this happen?" is a valid one, I'd rather turn attention away from the "why" and toward the "who" that endures. When I have paused to behold a person like Elizabeth, a person who has learned how to ride the tumultuous waves of life, I am usually humbled by what I see. More often than not, I see someone who is extraordinarily patient, exceptionally kind, and profoundly spiritual. True, tragedy and chronic heartbreak doesn't *necessarily* engender these qualities. I have likewise encountered individuals who are utterly broken by their pain, wrestling with anger or bitterness or, worse yet, *refusing* to wrestle with it and choosing instead to become sad, bitter, or sick people.

C. S. Lewis's classic novel *The Great Divorce* is an allegorical tale about a person who is journeying through the land between death and eternity. This place, Grey Town, can be either hell (if a person decides to remain) or purgatory (if the traveler

---

[1] See Gen 16:2; 25:21; 30:23; 1 Sam 1:1-18.

chooses to board the bus that goes "beyond the mountains" to heaven). As the narrator journeys along, he is accompanied by a spirit who helps him make sense of his experience. The spirit answers his questions, explaining the stories of the people who have chosen not to proceed to heaven but rather to remain forever in Grey Town, thus creating their own living hell. Upon encountering one such person, the narrator questions why she has been condemned:

> "That unhappy creature doesn't seem to me to be the sort of soul that ought to be even in danger of damnation. She isn't wicked: she's only a silly, garrulous old woman who has got into a habit of grumbling, and one feels that a little kindness, and rest, and change would put her all right."
>
> "That is what she once was. . . . The question is whether she is a grumbler, or only a grumble. If there is a real woman—even the least trace of one—still there inside the grumbling, it can be brought to life again. But if there's nothing but ashes we'll not go on blowing them in our own eyes forever." . . .
>
> "But how can there be a grumble without a grumbler?"
>
> ". . . it begins with a grumbling mood, and yourself still distinct from it: perhaps criticising it. And yourself, in a dark hour, may will that mood, embrace it. Ye can repent and come out of it again. But there may come a day when you can do that no longer. Then there will be no *you* left to criticise the mood, nor even to enjoy it, but just the grumble itself going on forever like a machine."[2]

The first time I read this, it chilled me to the bone, this deterioration from being a grumbler to becoming a grumble. It is perfectly natural to complain—even rage—about our hardships, and God is neither surprised nor hurt by our expressions of dismay, anger, or grief. Lament is an ancient biblical form of prayer bringing us into deeper relationship with God, not farther away. But when we cling to our hurt, allowing our pain

[2] C. S. Lewis, *The Great Divorce* (New York: Harper One, 1946), 76–78.

to corrode our relationship with God and others, we have traversed the distance from "grumbler" to "grumble," according to Lewis, and then we have tragically become someone infinitely less than our true self.

Elizabeth was no grumbler. Elizabeth was a woman who almost surely poured her heart out to God in lament over her barrenness. And then, in her old age, after accepting God's answer of no, she was granted her heart's desire—and then some. She was not only given a son who was a source of "joy and gladness," she was given the role of mothering a prophet who would "be great in the sight of the Lord." How did she respond? Much better than her husband did, that's for sure! His response of doubt literally kept him quiet for months (side point: never challenge an archangel. It can only end badly.). But Elizabeth said, "So has the Lord done for me at a time when he has seen fit to take away my disgrace before others." Her grief did not disappear; I even hesitate to say that it transformed. All those years of disappointment and humiliation were not taken away from Elizabeth, they just became a background piece of the bigger story. God hadn't finished writing her story yet, and the last few chapters would shed a completely different light on what had come before.

A colleague of mine who taught at a Catholic elementary school told me a story about one of her first graders, Rehan. As a young child coming from a devout Muslim family, he was just beginning to learn about Jesus in his religion classes. The teacher had set up a series of self-guided learning centers for the students to use independently while she worked with smaller reading groups. One of these centers held a simple book about the life of Jesus together with some felt figures the children could manipulate to re-create the story. One day as she was helping a group of readers, Rehan, with book in hand, excitedly interrupted her, "Look at what Jesus can do—he heals people and he tells great stories and he made wine out of plain old water!"

"Yes, Rehan, that's right. Now go on back to the center."

Not two minutes later, Rehan had returned. "This guy is amazing! He walked on water, did you know that?"

"Yes, Rehan, I did. Please read quietly so everyone can do their work."

Obediently, he returned to the center, only to reappear at her side soon after. "Hey, guess what? He wants everyone in the whole wide world to listen to him and learn how to love and forgive and do good works. Can I be his friend? Do you think I could be his friend?"

"Yes, of course you can be his friend. And do you know what Jesus would want right now? He would want you to keep reading about him quietly at the center. Can you do that?"

Rehan was so engrossed in the story he didn't return to the center, but plopped down right where he was and continued reading. Soon, he started to cry. The teacher noticed, looking to see what had happened. Rehan looked up at her and couldn't keep his emotion in.

"He died! Why did that happen? Why did they do that? Why did they kill him? He didn't do anything wrong. Why did he die?" he sputtered, inconsolable in his grief and confusion.

Seeing that his emotions were getting the better of him, she tried to soothe him, "Rehan, it's OK . . ." only to be interrupted with a gut-wrenched wail.

"No! They killed him and that was bad. He didn't do anything wrong. He was a good man. He was my friend!"

As he became increasingly distraught, the teacher had to raise her voice to get his attention: "Rehan, Rehan! Turn the page!"

He was too upset to finish the story himself, so gathering the reading group, she sat down next to him, and read the rest of the story aloud, narrating Jesus' resurrection from the dead. Rehan jumped up from the floor and started skipping around the room with squeals of elation: "He didn't stay dead! He didn't stay dead! Jesus got alive again!" he rejoiced, as the other students giggled at his antics.

Indeed, he did: Jesus got alive again. *That's* the end of the story. The story that starts on Good Friday doesn't end until Easter Sunday—it is one continuous narrative that begs not to be cut short.

Sadness, outrage, pain, injustice, grief—these are all very real, but they are not the end of the story. If we stay in these emotions and memories, we risk getting stuck in them, mired in darkness and bitterness, condemned to a life in Grey Town. What we need when we are on that threshold between "grumbling" and "grumble" is to be shaken out of the false belief that we've reached the end of the story. We need someone to remind us, insistently if necessary: *"Turn the page!"*

There is a land beyond grief and pain, but the only way to arrive at that land is *through* the valley of darkness and the shadow of death. Let us not be fooled into believing the lie that we are doomed—damned—to live forever in that dark valley of Grey Town. No. *No.* There *is* another side; God offers a different destination. And it is the place of resurrection where there is nothing more to grumble about—*ever*. There's only one hitch: we must choose to get on the bus and leave Grey Town—and all who inhabit it—behind us forever.

Elizabeth's final destination was becoming the mother of John the Baptist. She became the dwelling place of a miracle, the bearer of prophecy, and a vital participant in the plan of God for the salvation of the world. Beyond that, she became the first person to recognize the presence of God in her midst when she greeted her cousin Mary. She professed faith in what God had done—in herself and also in Mary—for the life of the world. Elizabeth honored Mary's "yes" to the God who had said "no" to her own prayer for so long. Elizabeth praised Mary's trust in the word of God, but when she cried out "blessed is she who believed that what the Lord said to her would be fulfilled," I can't help but wonder if she wasn't talking about her own blessing as well. Elizabeth addressed Mary as "she who believed," but I see this as a classic case of "it takes one to know one." Might this not be the exact reason Mary wanted to visit Elizabeth? Of all the people she could have seen, all the places she could have gone after Gabriel's annunciation of her pregnancy, she chose the safe haven of Elizabeth, one who also believed that the word of God would be fulfilled. Elizabeth was for Mary a place of refuge, of comfort, of homecoming. What a relief it must have been for Mary to hear the first words from Elizabeth: "Blessed are you!" Elizabeth understood. Elizabeth *knew*.

Who are your Elizabeths? The people who receive you with such warmth, such understanding, such belief in what God is doing in *you*? To have a person like this in our life is nothing short of a sheer blessing, and it would do us well to express gratitude for them—and ideally *to* them—regularly. Our Elizabeths recognize God's movements in us because they have had the experience of God working in their own lives— and, I daresay, in some instances of God seeming *not* to work in their lives. Elizabeth endured a near-lifetime of God's "no" before she ever experienced God's "yes" to her most vulnerable and heartfelt prayer, but when God turned that page, it changed the landscape of everything that had preceded it.

Her grief did not disappear from her life's history, but its hue changed dramatically. What had been humiliation, sadness, and ache suddenly, with the turning of the final page, became wonder, praise, and awe. Returning to *The Great Divorce*, the wise spirit guide expressed it best:

> "Son," he said, "ye cannot in your present state understand eternity . . . But ye can get some likeness of it if ye say that both good and evil, when they are full grown, become retrospective. Not only this valley but all this earthly past will have been Heaven to those who are saved. Not only the twilight in that town, but all their life on earth too, will then

be seen by the damned to have been Hell. That is what mortals misunderstand. . . . Both processes begin even before death. . . . That is why, at the end of all things, . . . the Blessed will say, 'We have never lived anywhere except in Heaven,' and the Lost, 'We were always in Hell.' And both will speak truly."[3]

From Elizabeth:

There is always more to your story. Sometimes it's mighty hard to believe. The darkness can be really, really dark, it's true, but take it from me: the darkness never wins. It's a pretty convincing liar, darkness. Combined with doubt, anger, grief, loss, betrayal, guilt, or shame, it will deceive you into thinking that it's won, that it has claimed victory over you, your happiness, your soul, your future. But don't you believe it, not for one minute. Don't you believe it. You come to me instead. Come visit me, and I'll tell you: *blessed are you*.

Yes, friend: *blessed are you who have believed*. Believe that there's more to your story than the grief. Believe, and keep praying. Oh, and turn the page. Then you'll see.

---

[3] Lewis, *Great Divorce*, 69.

Chapter 2: Joseph

Befriending Incompletion:
The Gift of Wonder

The death of Joseph

> Now this is how the birth of Jesus Christ came about. When his mother Mary was betrothed to Joseph, but before they lived together, she was found with child through the holy Spirit. Joseph her husband, since he was a righteous man, yet unwilling to expose her to shame, decided to divorce her quietly. Such was his intention when, behold, the angel of the Lord appeared to him in a dream and said, "Joseph, son of David, do not be afraid to take Mary your wife into your home. For it is through the holy Spirit that this child has been conceived in her. She will bear a son and you are to name him Jesus, because he will save his people from their sins." All this took place to fulfill what the Lord had said through the prophet:
>
>> "Behold, the virgin shall be with child and bear a son, and they shall name him Emmanuel,"
>
> which means "God is with us." When Joseph awoke, he did as the angel of the Lord had commanded him and took his wife into his home. He had no relations with her until she bore a son, and he named him Jesus.
>
> —*Matthew 1:18-25*

I consider Joseph a dear friend. In the Catholic world he is the patron saint for many types of folks: carpenters, stepfathers, refugees, home sellers (and home buyers as well, oddly), blended families, and women in labor. (That last one made me laugh out loud, as I imagine most women in labor would be loathe to invoke the intercession of a man who trekked his nine-month pregnant wife across the countryside on a donkey.) Beyond these traditional intercessory roles, however, Joseph has always been a much-needed anchor for me when I have been in situations involving "unfinished business." He, more than any other person I have encountered in the gospels, provides for me a sense of steadfastness. Joseph did not benefit from some of the predispositions Mary was supposedly given by God.[1] The Scriptures do not explicitly state that Joseph was divinely chosen for the role he was to fulfill; they merely say that he happened to be betrothed to the one who was! He was not sinless, he was not visited by the angel Gabriel as were Mary and Zechariah, he was not "full of grace" (Luke 1:5-38). He was, quite literally, just an ordinary Joe: 100 percent human, without overt predisposition for the role he was to play in salvation history.

Joseph is mentioned very few times in Scripture, and no word from him is recorded at all. He is present in the first two chapters of Matthew and Luke (for the annunciation of the birth of Jesus, the actual birth of Jesus, the flight to Egypt and the subsequent return to Nazareth, the presentation of the child Jesus in the temple, the finding of the adolescent Jesus in the temple, and in both gospels' genealogies). Mark makes no mention of him, and in John, we only hear of him when Jesus is derisively called the "son of Joseph" by those who questioned his authority.[2]

Who exactly was Joseph? According to the characterization in Matthew's gospel passage chosen for this chapter, he was these things:

- Engaged (v. 18)
- Righteous (v. 19)
- Discerning (v. 19)
- A dreamer (v. 20)

---

[1] Articles 488–93 of the *Catechism of the Catholic Church* refer to the agreement between Roman Catholicism and Eastern Orthodoxy that Mary was predestined to become the mother of the Savior, preserved from the moment of conception from the "stain of original sin" and, by the grace of God, remaining free from personal sin her whole life long.

[2] The complete list of these gospel references is Matt 1:1-16 (genealogy); Luke 3:23-38 (genealogy); Matt 1–2 (annunciation, birth, flight into Egypt, return to Nazareth); Luke 1–2 (annunciation, birth, presentation in the temple, finding in the temple); John 1:45, 6:42 (Jesus as the son of Joseph).

- A descendent of David (v. 20)
- A believer in prophecy (v. 23)
- Obedient to the word of God (v. 24)

If we were to look at this list of qualities out of context, we might not be very impressed (well, except maybe for the royal ancestry). Upon closer inspection, however, there is a hidden world of meaning to these characteristics when we put them all together in the person of Joseph.

First, he was engaged to be married to Mary. Betrothal for Jews of the first century typically lasted close to a year. During that time, the two people were considered husband and wife already, having completed the formal family arrangements, signed all the legal documents, and even exchanged rings—but they were not yet allowed any physical intimacy until the actual wedding celebration. The wedding ceremony could not occur until the groom had finished preparing a homestead for his new bride and she had finished preparing her trousseau. During those many months of preparation, the bride remained living with her parents, awaiting news that a wedding date had been set. It was in the course of this "in-between" time that Mary became pregnant with a baby Joseph knew was not his own.[3]

Joseph, of the line of King David, had inherited an extraordinary legacy, and he had built for himself over the course of his lifetime a reputation as a just and righteous man. He was a descendant not only of strong Jewish lineage but also of strong Jewish faith. The Torah texts about Abraham, Moses, and Elijah informed his living and working, and he likely knew the words of the psalms and prophets by heart. He was be-

---

[3] For a tremendous explication of the customs of the time and the social, religious, and cultural ramifications of Mary's pregnancy during the period of betrothal, I recommend Henry Skrzyński's book *The Jewess Mary, Mother of Jesus* (Kensington, Australia: Chevalier Press, 1994).

trothed to a young woman from a family of good reputation—faithful, hard-working, humble, observant—and odds are pretty good that he was looking forward with great hope to his forthcoming marriage.

Imagine, if you will, the moment when Joseph found out that Mary, his betrothed, was pregnant. It seems fair to imagine that confusion, disbelief, heartbreak, anger, and doubt may have come into play. Perhaps he felt cheated, deceived, or duped—by both Mary and God. And yet, he knew this woman . . .

How could this be? It can't be. But I see it with my own eyes—it is what it is. How can this possibly be? Was she attacked? She would not have done this on her own. Maybe it was a Roman soldier! But she is not protesting, not defending, not explaining . . . ? Oh, my heart!

Joseph, the just man. Joseph, the faithful man. Joseph, the husband of Mary. He knew that if he accused her of infidelity, it would amount to an indictment of adultery, resulting in the legal consequence of Mary's death by public stoning. He was "unwilling to expose her to shame," this woman whom he loved so much. And yet, exactly *because* he was faithful and righteous, he also could not marry a woman who had sinned in such a way. It is difficult to imagine the crisis of soul Joseph experienced in those days of uncertainty, but it is not difficult to imagine the intensity of his prayer. The result of his discernment was the decision to "divorce her quietly," which meant that he would break off the marriage without accusing her of infidelity. If there were no accusation from the husband, there could be no attribution of adultery. He would simply remain silent, a final expression of his love for her, which also allowed him to remain unwaveringly faithful to God.

"Such was his intention when, behold, the angel of the Lord appeared to him in a dream."

Now wait just a minute. Mary was *visited* by an angel (an *arch*angel, by the way, named Gabriel). But Joseph had a *dream* about an angel visit? What, was Gabriel's schedule all full up that day? Did Joseph not meet the proper qualifications for an archangelic visit?

Joseph had a dream, and when he woke up, he took its message as (sorry for the pun) gospel truth. Let me ask you, dear reader: have you ever had a dream that was so real that you woke up and it took a minute before you realized it hadn't actually happened? I certainly have. Given a little bit of time, daylight, and coffee, however, I was able to distinguish dream from reality. But Joseph and his dream? He concluded that the instruction from the angel in his dream *was* real life, and he determined to live in accord with it.[4]

This is phenomenal. *Phe-nom-e-nal.*

Throughout the course of her life, Mary had proof in her body that her experience with the angel Gabriel had been real, true, and trustworthy. What Gabriel said God would do, God *did* do, and what was inexplicable to human reasoning, utterly extraordinary, proved itself believable by the very child growing in her womb. What did Joseph have? Joseph had a dream. Add to that nothing more than the word of the woman he loved and his faith in the God he believed in. What else did he have? *Constant, steadfast trust.* And it was enough.

So Joseph awakened from his dream and acted on it. He did exactly as the angel instructed and kept Mary as his wife. That might sound like a nice fairytale ending to a relatively tense moment of crisis, but in reality, this would have been yet

---

[4] A bit of scriptural context is in order here. The gospel writer intended his original audience (Jewish Christians) to draw a connection between Joseph, the husband of Mary, and their father in faith, Jacob's favored son, "Joseph, the master dreamer" (cf. Gen 37). Throughout the entirety of Matthew's gospel, we encounter parallels between Jesus and his Old Testament forebears, and it begins with this connection of his foster father Joseph to the most important figures in Israel's history—first through the genealogy and then through an angel who appeared to Joseph in a dream, addressing him as "son of David." As a result of this dream, Joseph directly participated in God's plan for salvation history—just like his namesake from Genesis had done.

another crisis in the cultural context of first-century Judaism. Since Joseph did not accuse Mary but instead went through with the wedding, accepting her as his bride, the community would have drawn the only logical conclusion: Joseph was the father of the baby. How is that a crisis, you ask, given the fact that they were already betrothed? Remember, during the betrothal time, physical intimacy was not allowed. Therefore, Joseph accepted Mary into his home and subsequently accepted the communal verdict that he was not at all a "just and righteous man" but a hypocrite and a scoundrel. His faithfulness to the word of God ironically gave the appearance of faithlessness—and sin. *And he knew it would be as such.* Loving Mary, protecting Jesus, and being faithful to the call of God (obscure as it was—in a *dream*!) cost him his good reputation, the trust of the community he loved, and the near picture-perfect future he likely had in mind for himself and his bride.

No two ways about it: *Joseph is a dude*. And not just any dude, but a dude of the highest caliber, at least in my book.

OK, so if the dream wasn't the fairytale ending, then surely being foster father to the incarnate Son of God must be. Right? From our point of view, yes. From Joseph's? Let's ponder this a little more deeply.

The words of the angel in the dream were most certainly confirmed by the subsequent conversations he and Mary must have had about who Jesus was and how he came to be. The visit of the Magi: further confirmation. All throughout those first months, Joseph may well have had his trust bolstered, his faith confirmed. As a man of strong belief and genuine goodness, his prayer must have been one of wonder and awe at the role he was given to play, at the privilege of raising the Son of God and his mother Mary. But Scripture falls silent between Jesus' infancy and adolescence, and those "hidden years" are visible only in our imagination. Joseph taught Jesus what he knew—lessons of God, of faith, of history, of family, of tradesmanship. And surely Jesus learned how to be a good man from

Joseph, as well as how to be a good Jew, a good son, and a good disciple. But there's one little detail that has always bothered me, and it's this: the incompleteness of Joseph's experience.

The last time Joseph appears in Scripture is in Luke 2:41-50, when Jesus was twelve years old and was inadvertently left behind in Jerusalem (side note: any parent can relate to the panic and terror of the experience of losing a child in a crowd, but imagine Mary and Joseph's alarm at the realization that they had lost the Son of God!) After the resolution of this incident (whew!) the next set of "hidden years" occurs, lasting until Jesus began his public ministry at the age of thirty. Those eighteen years of Jesus' life between the age of twelve and thirty must have held many things, but one of them was most certainly the death of Joseph.

Incompletion.

Before his death, what did Joseph know of his son, Jesus? He had a dream in which an angel told him that the baby born of Mary would save the world from sin because he would be the long-awaited Emmanuel. He witnessed the Magi presenting Jesus with rare gifts while offering homage and telling tales of a star that signified the birth of a great king. He had another dream warning him of impending threat to the life of Jesus and instructing him to take the family and flee to Egypt. A third dream instructed him to return safely to Israel after the death of Herod. Then, when he and Mary found Jesus at age twelve in the temple, he was astonishing the religious teachers with his understanding and knowledge of the Scriptures.

Maybe I'm missing something, but nowhere in there do I see—or can I even infer—that "Jesus revealed himself to be the Messiah that Joseph long-believed he was," or even something as simple as "Jesus assured Joseph that everything he had believed about his identity as the Son of God was true." Nope. Joseph didn't have all the verifying data. He died before Jesus was manifested as anything other than "the son of Joseph." He died while Jesus was still living at home, working and living as one of the community. He died believing in the faithfulness of God, the power of love, and the trustworthiness of dreams—but without seeing any of it definitively revealed.

This is why I consider Joseph a dear friend. He is the patron saint of all things unfinished. And he offers us an alternative to perfect completion: *wonder*.

The word "wonder" can be used in a variety of ways. We wonder whether or not the forecasted rain will arrive as predicted, and we wonder what might have happened if Jack and Rose had shared the driftwood at the end of the movie *Titanic*. Wonder can describe our speculation about something uncertain or our skepticism about something dubious, but it can also describe a sense of awe at something marvelous. We *wonder* at the majesty and beauty of the Grand Canyon or at the delicacy of a newborn baby's tiny fingers and toes. This is the wonder of Joseph. When he reached the end of his life and Jesus' messianic storyline hadn't yet come to completion, I'm guessing Joseph did then what he had consistently done every day of his life before then—he sat in wonder at the workings of God in and around him.

At the church I attend in St. Louis, there is a bas-relief marble depiction of the death of Joseph. The first time I saw it, it took my breath away. Joseph is central to the work, with Mary and Jesus on either side, each one holding his hand. Joseph is slightly reclined as he tilts his head upward, Mary is sadly but peacefully looking at Jesus, and Jesus has his eyes fixed on Joseph as he points upward to the heavens as if to say, "It's all true, Dad. It's all true."[5] Joseph, a man so faithful and faith-filled, so trusting and patient, left this world before it knew the Son of God was his son, too. Joseph helps me loosen

---

[5] A simple Google image search for "death of St. Joseph" provides a wide variety of artistic renderings of the imagined scene. The bas-relief I mention is from St. Francis Xavier College Church at Saint Louis University, pictured at the start of this chapter, and can be seen at https://youtu.be/nddBUkAX1cs?t=274.

my grip on things I don't want to release, encouraging me to sit in wonder at the possibilities that open up when I actually do let go.

"*Try it,*" he counsels. "*Trust it.*"

When we choose to wonder at the miracle of what *has been* and the possibility of what *yet to be* instead of worrying over how things might turn out, or brooding over what *might have been*, we find ourselves making peace with what may always remain incomplete. If we spend our time waiting for tidy conclusions, we will condemn ourselves to a lifetime of angst and disappointment. Only when we treasure life *as it is happening* will we experience the fullness of its beauty. Hans Urs von Balthasar says it best in my favorite spiritual work, *Heart of the World*, excerpted here:

> Perfection lies in the fullness of journey. For this reason, never think you have arrived. Forget what lies behind you; reach out for what lies before you. Through the very change in which you lose what you have snatched up, you will at last be transformed into what you crave for with such longing. . . . [Y]ou cannot interrupt music in order to catch and hoard it. Let it flow and flee, otherwise you cannot grasp it. You cannot condense it into one beautiful chord and thus possess it once and for all. Patience is the first virtue of the one who wants to perceive. And the second is renunciation.[6]

Or, put a different way: patience + renunciation = wonder.

There is one last word to say about the gift of wonder in Joseph's life. The possibility that Jesus might have revealed *something* of his divinity to Joseph before he died is a comforting one for me, providing at least a bit of closure and comfort. But then what? According to Christian theology, it was at

---

[6] Hans Urs von Balthasar, *Heart of the World* (San Francisco: Ignatius Press, 1979), 23–24.

his own death and resurrection that Jesus Christ "opened the gates of heaven."[7] So when Joseph died, heaven's gates were still "closed." Even his eternal story remained unfinished! Yes, even in death, Joseph waited. He waited in wonder for his son's resurrection just as in life he had waited for his son's revelation.

See why I claim that Joseph is a dude? Through the entirety of his life—and even after—Joseph believed and waited in wonder. And isn't it lovely to imagine that when Jesus opened those heavenly gates, he walked through them to greet God his Father, arm-in-arm with Joseph his dad.

From Joseph:

Well, I don't have much to say, I'm afraid. What you need to know, you can learn from my boy. But I'll tell you this much: being his earthly dad was amazing. Sure, it's easy to say that in retrospect, but I remember every single one of those days I was with him and his mother. How lucky I was, blessed be God. It wasn't all easy, and there are plenty of things I could have done differently, better probably. But none of it matters much. What matters now is the only thing that mattered then, when I could stay still enough to notice: Emmanuel, God-with-us. God was with us *every single day*! And, wonder of wonders, I named him Jesus, and he called me dad.

---

[7] *Catechism of the Catholic Church*, 2nd ed. (Washington, DC: United States Catholic Conference—Libreria Editrice Vaticana, 199), article 637.

Chapter 3: Andrew

Befriending Second Place: The Gift of Perspective

St. Andrew and St. Peter

The next day John [the Baptist] was there again with two of his disciples, and as he watched Jesus walk by, he said, "Behold, the Lamb of God." The two disciples heard what he said and followed Jesus. Jesus turned and saw them following him and said to them, "What are you looking for?" They said to him, "Rabbi," (which translated means Teacher) "where are you staying?" He said to them,

"Come, and you will see." So they went and saw where he was staying, and they stayed with him that day. It was about four in the afternoon.

Andrew, the brother of Simon Peter, was one of the two who heard John and followed Jesus. He first found his own brother Simon and told him, "We have found the Messiah" (which is translated Anointed). Then he brought him to Jesus.

—*John 1:35-42a*

Recently, a new publication hit the bookstores and became an instant bestseller. *Spare*, the (first?) memoir by Prince Harry, Duke of Sussex, broke the Guinness World Record for the fastest-selling non-fiction book of all time, selling on its date of release over 1.4 million copies in the United Kingdom and the United States alone.[1] When I first heard of it, I did not understand the title reference, so I did some homework. According to a BBC article written just three days prior to the book's release, "The saying 'an heir and a spare' refers to aristocratic families needing an heir to inherit a title or an estate, and the 'spare' as the younger sibling who could be the replacement if anything happened to the heir before he or she has their own children."[2] This little snippet not only gave me an appreciation of the book title, but it also evoked in me a strong sense of sympathy, mingled with a good dose of sadness.

---

[1] Sanj Atwal, "Prince Harry's Spare Becomes Fastest-Selling Non-Fiction Book Ever," *Guinness World Records* (January 13, 2023), available at https://www.guinnessworldrecords.com/news/2023/1/prince-harrys-spare-becomes-fastest-selling-non-fiction-book-ever-732915.

[2] Sean Coughlin, "The Enduring Anguish of Being the Royal 'Spare,'" *BBC News* online (January 7, 2023), available at https://www.bbc.com/news/uk-64185317.

What does it mean to be "the spare," second fiddle, benchwarmer, understudy, back-up plan? How does one make sense of their life when it is defined in relationship to someone else's success—or even their mere existence? Books, movies, and artwork have explored this question through the ages, bidding us reckon with the discomfort such reflection brings.[3] Granted, there is nobility (and even fame) in some areas—ghost writers, for example, or stage crew, or stunt doubles—but when the experience of coming in just behind someone else comes 'round, it doesn't feel quite so glorious. (Anyone who can conjure up a dreadful memory of grade school playgrounds where they were one of the last teammates chosen has a sense of this feeling.) The feeling of *almost* being chosen, but ultimately being left out is a feeling that demands something of us.

Enter Andrew.

The Gospel of John is clear: Andrew met Jesus first and then went to get his brother Simon. Luke tells us that the first time Jesus encountered Simon Peter was after an unsuccessful fishing expedition with James and John, and that "when they brought their boats to the shore, they left everything and followed him" (Luke 5:11). Most every time we meet Andrew in the gospels, he is bringing someone to Jesus. Who brought the boy with the loaves and the fishes when everyone else had basically lamented the impossibility of the situation? Andrew. When a group of Greeks (i.e., pagans) told Philip they wanted to meet Jesus, guess who was enlisted to bring them to Jesus? Andrew. (See John 6:8-9; 12:22.)

Andrew's faith and leadership seem obvious from these passages, as they likely also were to his contemporaries. Andrew was someone who could get things done. He listened to John the Baptist's encouragement to follow Jesus—and then did so. He was convinced after that brief amount of time that

---

[3] Consider the characters of Salieri in *Amadeus*, Anna Fitzgerald in *My Sister's Keeper*, or even Van Gogh's *Portrait of Doctor Gachet*.

Jesus was truly the Messiah and immediately went to summon his brother Peter.

The brothers Andrew and Peter were fishermen partners with the brothers James and John, familiar to one another long before meeting Jesus (Luke 5:10). Yet, several Scripture passages indicate that Jesus chose *three* out of these four to be with him in certain significant moments in his life—with Andrew being the one left out. Why? There is no record in the gospels of Andrew denying Jesus like Peter did (Luke 22:31-34, 54-62), no account of Andrew jockeying for position among the Twelve like James and John (Mark 10:35-38). Andrew listened, heeded, discerned, proclaimed, and brought people straight to Jesus. Not a bad legacy, in my opinion. So why wasn't Andrew part of Jesus' "inner circle"? Why did he seem to disappear into the background so quickly? As the life and ministry of Jesus started to take shape and pick up speed, Jesus invited Peter, James, and John to be with him in moments of great vulnerability. Let's look at these incidents in chronological order from the Gospel of Mark:

- Relatively early in the ministry and teaching of Jesus, he encountered a synagogue official, Jairus, whose daughter was very ill. Jesus went to Jairus's home and subsequently raised the girl from the dead. At the moment of his entry into the house, "he did not allow anyone to accompany him inside except Peter, James, and John" (Mark 5:37).

- At one of the most intimate spiritual moments of his life, the Transfiguration, Jesus went to Mount Tabor and selected his companions deliberately: "Jesus took Peter, James, and John and led them up a high mountain apart by themselves" (Mark 9:2).

- And then Gethsemane, the agony in the garden on the last night of his life. At this most vulnerable moment, "he took with him Peter, James, and John and began to be troubled and distressed" (Mark 14:33).

I cannot read or hear these gospel passages without noticing Andrew's absence, without feeling a little bit let down by the invitation to just Peter, James, and John. Was this Andrew's emotional experience? We can never know, but the reflection is worth the effort.

Consider for a moment your own experience of being left out from a friend's invitation to something meaningful in their life. What are the feelings that bubble up? What are the immediate words that rise to the surface of your thinking? I can imagine a variety of possibilities, and none of them feels very good. But is there something else there, too?

My parents raised thirteen children (no, that's not a typo) in a relatively small St. Louis home. At one point, they had twelve children in the house, none of them yet old enough for high school. Dinner was a daily ordeal for my mother—deciding on what it would be, shopping for the ingredients, preparing the food, cooking it, serving it, cleaning up, and then starting the cycle all over for the next day's dinner. My mom was particularly skilled at arranging those meals to be economical, nutritious, and not all that bad tasting, but variety was not her strong suit. I imagine that given her need to focus on volume and efficiency, she had to sacrifice creativity. This would explain the predictable nature of most meals—a tall stack of white bread planted each night in the center of the table, a pitcher of milk (a mixture of whole milk and icky powdered milk that made the whole concoction foamy) within arm's reach of the oldest, some sort of meat, vegetable, and starch. Mondays we ate chicken; Fridays fish; Saturdays were for leftovers or pot pies. When she was in her retirement years, I would often ask her about those early days and the experiences of raising and feeding all those kids. Whenever I would ask her to tell me about a "normal day," she would shake her head and say something like, "Oh, Virginia Marie, I don't know. All those years were a blur. I was just trying to keep you children fed and clothed and all in one piece. I don't remember details. Except one night . . ." And then she would proceed to chuckle a bit as a memory emerged, launching her into a story. This was one of my favorites:

> *Wednesday nights we often had spaghetti. All you kids loved spaghetti, so I knew I wouldn't have to fight anyone to clean their plates. I was standing at the stove to dish out the portions, ready to load a mountain of noodles and sauce on whatever plate was handed to me from the horde of children gathered around. I didn't want anyone too close to the fire, so I was ignoring the commotion from the throng. Each child was trying to get closest, holding their plate to me and calling, "Me first!" "Me first!" "Me first!" As I got the first spoonful of spaghetti ready to dish out, I heard a voice from somewhere in the bunch say, "Me second!" and it tickled my funny bone. I looked around to see who that enterprising youngster was, and there was five-year-old John, all the way at the back, throwing a Hail Mary pasta pass and hoping it might win the day. I don't know who I served first that night, but I sure do remember that lopsided grin when I took his plate from him and handed it back saying, "Here you go, 'you second.'"*

Not coming in first isn't all bad, it turns out. It's all about your perspective! Let's reconsider Andrew. It's true, he doesn't seem to be selected for special consideration by Jesus the same way as Peter, James, and John, but if we shift perspective on this just a bit, we may be surprised at what we see.

I had the good fortune to live in Kaohsiung, Taiwan, for three years teaching English to elementary school and middle school children. During that time, I came to learn the basics of the Mandarin Chinese language. At daily Mass, I would follow along in the missal, trying to match the written characters with the oral language being spoken by priest and congregation. One day, as the priest was proclaiming the gospel passage above, where Andrew met Jesus and brought Peter to him, I heard something that stopped me in my tracks. I was so stunned that I had to backtrack to make sure I wasn't making one of my oh-so-common translation mistakes. Sure enough, there it was in the text: "Andrew, the older brother of Simon Peter, one of the two who followed Jesus after hearing what John had said . . ."[4]

Wait, what? "*Older* brother? That can't be right," I thought. Sure enough, though, in the next verse: "[Andrew] went to find his *younger brother* Simon."[5]

I sat through the remainder of the Mass unable to concentrate on anything except this arresting new concept to me: that Andrew may have been the big brother and Peter the little brother. Neither the English nor the original Greek translation indicates birth order. The Chinese is unambiguous, however, since the word for "younger brother" (弟弟, pronounced "dee-dee") and the word for "older brother" (哥哥, pronounced "guh-guh") are completely different words.[6] I had always had a mental construct of Peter as the elder of the two brothers,[7] so I consulted the most trustworthy local source of Chinese Christian theology I knew: Cardinal Paul Shan.[8] When I asked him about this interpretation of Peter as the younger brother to Andrew, Cardinal Shan looked as puzzled at my question as I had felt sitting in the chapel earlier. He gently reminded

---

[4] 西滿伯多祿的哥哥安得德肋, 就是聽了若翰的話 (John 1:40).

[5] 先去找到了自己的弟弟西滿 (John 1:41).

[6] I am indebted to my friends Benedict Sher, 佘祥磊, and Grace Chiang, 江弘禎, for providing the Chinese texts for these passages and for indulging more cultural questions from me than any human being should have to endure.

[7] European art commonly depicts Peter as older, exemplified in works such as Matteo di Giovanni's *The Calling of Saints Peter and Andrew* (circa 1470) and Fernando Gallego's *St. Andrew and St. Peter* (circa 1480, pictured at the start of this chapter).

[8] Paul Shan Kuo-hsi, SJ, 單國璽, was the bishop emeritus of Kaohsiung, Taiwan, during the years I lived there. Cardinal Shan was born in mainland China, taking his vows as a Jesuit priest in Beijing in 1948. He earned a theological doctorate in Rome and served in the Philippines and Vietnam before being named to church leadership in Taiwan, where he served from 1963 until his death in 2012. His biography can be found on the Vatican's website at https://www.vatican.va/news_services/press/documentazione/documents/cardinali_biografie/cardinali_bio_shan-kuo-hsi_p_en.html.

me that the original first century texts do not specify seniority, leaving themselves open to speculation. The Chinese translation follows the pattern of the Hebrew Scriptures, wherein the younger son is often the one singled out for a special role in salvation history. His answer went something like this:

Consider the multitude of stories from Genesis—Abel, younger brother to Cain, is the favored one; Isaac, the younger brother of Ishmael, is chosen by Abraham; Jacob, younger brother of Esau, gains Isaac's blessing; Joseph, younger brother to Jacob's other sons, is his favorite. Also consider Moses, Gideon, Solomon—all younger brothers. And perhaps the most astounding of all—King David, youngest and least impressive of Jesse's eight sons. Consider also the parable of the prodigal son: Jesus crafts the parable to make the younger son the main character. Doesn't it follow reason to think that Peter, singled out by Jesus for leadership among the Twelve, would be the younger son?[9]

Oh.

I distinctly remember sitting across from Cardinal Shan just sort of blinking in his general direction with my mouth hanging open. He was clearly amused at my speechlessness and said, "If I recall correctly, you, too, are the youngest in your family?"

Why yes, yes I am.

I pondered then, and I have continued to ponder since, why exactly this recasting of the persons of Andrew and Peter is so consequential to me. I think it's because it changes my perspective. It alters the way I perceive Andrew—specifically in what I perceive to be the experience of being "left out" of Jesus' inner circle of Peter, James, and John. I, of course, begin from the context of being the youngest child in a very large

---

[9] It is imperative at least to acknowledge the patriarchal norms evident here which may offend our contemporary sensibilities of equity and justice.

family of origin. With twelve older siblings, all of whom have always been very accomplished, very respected, and very *kind* people, I know what it's like to feel small and insignificant. As a kid, I always wanted to play the games the older ones were playing, hang out with their friends when they came to the house, go out to the events they were attending. More often than not, though, I was too little. Don't get me wrong—they did include me when they could. My sister Rose would read with me every night, sitting with me in the big squeaky living room rocking chair and patiently enduring every possible adventure of Clifford the Big Red Dog. And my brother Joe finally caved to my incessant pleas to join the kickball game in our alley by agreeing, "Fine, you can be second base." (Although I feel it necessary to include the small detail that he did not mean I could *play the position* of second base, but that I could actually *be* second base by replacing the frisbee that marked the location to tag.) The point is that as the youngest in the family, I was always intent on being included, constantly working to measure up. If Peter was the younger brother to Andrew, I can imagine Peter looking up to Andrew, modelling himself on the person Andrew was—as a fisherman, as a person of faith, and as a disciple of Jesus. I imagine Peter being immensely grateful to Andrew for the introduction to Jesus. And I notice that Andrew, as an older brother, recognized in Peter the leadership, humility, and honesty that would later translate into Jesus' own authority after his death.

My oldest sister Helen and oldest brother Paul headed up the herd that was the Herbers family. (As a matter of fact, they continue to do so!) As kids growing up at the front end of such a big family, they had responsibility thrust upon them from the earliest of ages. Among numerous other chores, Helen was leader of the dirty diaper patrol and Paul was captain of shoe-shining every Sunday night. The responsibilities they carried, together with the heavy expectations of setting a good example for the rest of the kids, could have led them to become a lot of things—resentful, rebellious, apathetic, absent, or even cruel. Instead, these two people chose goodness, generosity, reliability, and humor. Beginning with diapers and shoes, and then continuing with tutoring, babysitting, and a variety of other roles, Helen and Paul charted a course for the rest of us that actually formed the family dynamic. Because of the example they set (combined with a more-than-average spirit of competition,) a family culture was formed around education, service, story-telling, and integrity. My parents formed their children, but it was the older siblings who showed the rest of us how to step up and become the people my parents hoped we would be.

Could the same have been true for Andrew and Peter as brothers? We don't know who was younger or who was older, and I suppose it doesn't really matter. If Andrew was the younger brother watching from a distance as Peter, James, and John went off with Jesus now and then, maybe he did so with a sense of awe and admiration, continuing to learn faithfulness from his big brother. And if Andrew was the older brother, watching from a distance as Peter, James, and John went off with Jesus now and then, maybe he did so with a sense of pride and gratitude, happy to know that his kid brother was getting it right. Regardless of what was true of their birth order, we know one thing for sure: both Andrew and Peter were invited by Jesus to follow him, a call known by only a very special few. Andrew might not have been one of Jesus' "inner circle of three," but he was one of the twelve apostles—one of the first, in fact, to recognize Jesus as the Messiah. It would serve us well to keep that—and him—in perspective.

From Andrew:

What a silly question. Did it bother me to be left out? Boy, that's not the way I see it at all. This is how I see it: I was following John the Baptist, and I was ready for a lifetime of discipleship to him. He was something else—so charismatic, inspiring, faith-filled! And then one day, he pointed to Jesus and said, "Him. Follow him. He's the one we've been waiting for." So I did. I trusted him and I did it. That was a funny day, actually, when Jesus finally turned around and said, "What do you two want, anyway?" or something like that. I just kind of stammered, "Where are you going?" and he invited us to join him. He spoke and it was like John's charisma multiplied seventy times seven. It was so clear to me that John was right—Jesus was the one we'd been waiting for. He was the Messiah. And I knew immediately that I needed to get Peter. After listening to Jesus for just a few hours, I knew two things with regard to my brother: one, that he would want to follow Jesus just like I did; and two, that Peter's qualities were a perfect match to the kingdom Jesus was describing.

Was I jealous? Maybe I would have been if we were kids, vying over pieces of candy, but Jesus isn't candy. We don't have to share Jesus—he gives all of himself to each one of us. Every single day. So it's not about being his favorite, really. It's simply about being *his*.

Chapter 4: Martha

Befriending Worry: The Gift of Reverence

Martha reproving her sister Mary

As they continued their journey he entered a village where a woman whose name was Martha welcomed him. She had a sister named Mary who sat beside the Lord at his feet listening to him speak. Martha, burdened with much serving, came to him and said, "Lord, do you not care that my sister has left me by myself to do the serving? Tell her to help me." The Lord said to her in reply, "Martha, Martha, you are anxious and worried about many things. There is need of only one thing. Mary has chosen the better part and it will not be taken from her."

—*Luke 10:38-42*

So many thoughts. I have heard and read this passage more times than I can count, and each time I have a different internal response, depending, of course, on whatever is happening in the rest of my life at that particular point in time. I have felt scolded by it, I have gotten defensive about it, wept over it, and snorted at it. Pause here for a moment, re-read the brief passage again, and really identify your emotional response right now.

First, a question: do you find yourself taking someone's side in this story? Are you rooting for Martha? Understanding of Mary? Compassionate toward Jesus? Maybe you find yourself taking someone's side in a different sense—are you feeling protective of Mary's contemplation at the feet of Jesus or are you feeling aggravated with her, like Martha seemed to be? Are you trying to understand what Jesus is saying about Mary or are you annoyed that he hasn't recognized Martha's need for help? Are you more likely to find yourself at Martha's shoulder thinking, "Yeah, Lord, tell Mary to get in gear!" or at Mary's shoulder thinking, "She's right here, you know, you can speak directly to Mary instead of tattling to Jesus." I have never had any trouble imagining this scene. Regardless of my sympathetic leanings, I always envision the same setting: Martha, hands on her hips, in an apron looking haggard, Jesus sitting at the hearth looking worn and tired, and Mary seated on the floor looking completely oblivious. (This is not intended to be a criticism of Mary. As the youngest in my family and often accused of being spoiled as a child, I am quite familiar with the "completely oblivious" look.) The scene, however, cannot be watered down to a simple case of sisterly spatting.

It is never advisable to isolate a single Scripture passage and attempt to understand it without knowing its full context: what came beforehand, what the setting was, who was involved, and what the gospel writers might have intended for their audience. Let's start with who is involved here. This passage is a private exchange, not a teaching of Jesus, not a parable, not a healing, not a miracle. It is a simple exchange inside Martha's home (read verse 38 again: *Martha's* home). A very brief conversation is recorded—one that leaves none of the three folks involved coming off looking very good. Martha seems a little rude, Mary seems a little lazy, and Jesus seems a little unappreciative! So let's ask the first question: what in the world is this exchange doing in the gospel?! How did it "make the cut" for the author of Luke's gospel who, by the way, wasn't even there? Who kept this story alive in oral tradition before it was written down in gospel form—and why? Scripture scholars agree that this home in Bethany was a place that Jesus visited often—presumably because Martha, Mary, and Lazarus (three siblings) were close friends of his. That makes Martha and Mary trusted confidantes in this story, not just hostesses of an honored guest. Jesus has come to a place that felt like home to him.

But where has he come from?

This conversation is set in the tenth chapter of Luke's gospel, which marks a significant turning point in the public life of Jesus. Prior to this, Jesus had been calling disciples to himself, preaching, healing, teaching, forgiving, exorcising, feeding multitudes, calming storms, and finally making dire predictions about the way all of it would end—with his own rejection and ultimately death. With the start of chapter 10,

Jesus' instructions to his followers become increasingly foreboding. He speaks about the cost of discipleship, the reversal of power structures, the difference between ritual observance and authentic faithfulness, and the hypocrisy of the religious elite. To put it simply, having won over the sick, the sinner, and the stigmatized, he is now quickly alienating the powerful, the pretentious, and the pharisaical. Moreover, in the final section of chapter 9, he has "resolutely determined to journey to Jerusalem" (v. 51), setting his face staunchly in the direction of opposition and treachery. He is single-minded in his purpose and mission, fully aware that Jerusalem is not just the place where they are going; it is the place where his journey on earth will end—badly.

It is in the course of *this* journey that he arrived at Martha's house.

The text indicates that he arrived alone. Given the context outlined above, he likely arrived weary, not just from his travels but perhaps more so from the toll of preaching unpopular messages, engaging with resistant audiences, and explaining misunderstood lessons (which must have been especially wearying when that explanation was required by his closest followers). He arrived in Bethany at a place of refuge, a home of friends, closing the door behind him and sitting down with what I imagine was a sigh of both relief and respite. And Mary sat down with him, sensing his need, prepared to listen to him.

Then there's our friend Martha. Oh, Martha . . . can't you just hear her? "Jesus is here! What is there to serve him? Do I have any fresh bread? Where's the wine? Oh, why didn't I sweep up this morning? We need to clean the plates, stoke the fire, shake the crumbs off the linens! Oh heavens, what is that noise? He needs rest—we need to tell the neighbors to pipe down. He must be hungry, what might he like to eat? Is it cool enough in here? Should I open the doors? Do I have time to get to the market for some fresh fruit? Where is that sister of mine? There's so much to do—Jesus is here!"

In my imagination, I can easily sense the flurry of activity, recognizing the age-old fretting that emerges in such circumstances, even two thousand years later. Martha is not mistaken—the food does need to be prepared, the table set, the needs of everyone met. There is plenty of serving that must be done. Maybe just *not right now*. As *she* makes the determination of what Jesus needs, she neglects to see what's most important to *him* at the moment. Her "burden of serving" (see v. 40) is self-imposed, as are the worry and anxiety that result from it. Does he need to eat? Eventually—but first, he needs to be heard. Mary apparently recognized which needs came first—the need of friendship, the need of coming home. Her recognition prompted her to sit down, leave the serving to later, and listen to her friend. Martha, however, was distracted by what she imagined Jesus must want—and so she "fretted and stewed," as my mother was fond of saying.

Her blindness to Jesus' actual need was so complete, however, that she actually attempted to enlist him as arbiter in her grievance against her sister. What might she have been expecting Jesus to say in response to her plea? "Mary, shame on you! Look at what needs to be done. Can't you see how Martha is doing *everything*? Go help her!" In point of fact, it seems Martha actually *interrupted* Jesus in order to ask him to play referee. (Don't believe me? Read it again.)

Ever so gently, Jesus responded. Over time, I have come to understand this passage as a healing miracle, for I truly believe that in this exchange, Jesus removed the blindness caused by Martha's worry. He began by calling her name, confirming their relationship—she was beloved to him. "Martha, Martha . . ." Then, he named her malady: "You are anxious and worried about many things." Ah, yes . . . a common malady—and contagious! Then, the healing which came in the form of a reminder of what she had forgotten due to her worry: "There is need of only one thing." Interestingly, Jesus didn't specifically name the "one thing," but he did say that Mary had discovered and chosen it. What had she chosen? What was that "one thing"? Jesus himself. Presence. Attentiveness. Time. Reverence.

Although the gospel doesn't continue, I imagine him saying, "Sit down, Martha. Sit and be with me. That's why I'm here. We'll figure out dinner later. For now, please just come. I don't care if the house is dirty or hot or loud. I just want to be with you. Please come. Please sit."

And there she is: apron-clad Martha, hands on her hips, mouth still open, blinking into the silence that waits for her response, able to see what has suddenly become visible to her—*the one thing necessary.*

The gospel story ends there, but certainly the experience did not. What happened next, do you think? Well, I'll tell you what *didn't* happen. There is no recorded "Miracle of the Loaves and Dishes" where the bread miraculously got baked and the plates were made clean. So what did happen? It seems reasonable to assume that they eventually ate a meal together (prepared hopefully as a joint sisterly effort), but before that, it likewise seems reasonable to assume that Martha sat down next to her sister at the feet of Jesus, focused on him and his words. Having laid down the burden of worry and anxiety, Martha learned reverence.

In my mind's eye, this is a gospel moment of great beauty and joy. (Imagine Jesus choosing my home—*my home!*—to come and find rest.) It is also, however, a gospel moment that convicts me. I am often standing burdened with Martha, hands on hips, imploring God to dispense divine justice to all those sitting on their duffs while I'm busy tending to all that needs to be done. What "needs" to be done seems so clear, so obvious, and I am confounded by those who are not responding. I can easily identify the needs of the given situation and I just as easily respond with the quickness of activity and worry. Then, I hear God's response: *Virginia, Virginia, you are anxious and worried about so many things. There is need of only one thing.* Only one thing.

The dozens of things that "need to be done" do indeed need to be done, granted, but has my worry and anxiety over them blinded me to the presence of God right in my midst? I stand with mouth agape and it starts to dawn on me, "Oh, yeah. I'm missing the point." In that moment, I am invited—by God or by Martha, I'm not sure who—to close my mouth, take off the apron, put down the accusations, and be in God's presence. Notice. Listen. Revere.

Years ago, the father of a friend of mine had a debilitating stroke, necessitating complete care for several months of his early recovery. The stroke affected his entire body, initially keeping him bedridden and unable to care for even his most basic needs. Every day my friend would visit him, first at the hospital and then at the rehab center. As a single mom of young children who also held a demanding full-time job, the only time she had to spend with her dad was during her lunch hour. She would arrive in a flurry, hoping to have at least thirty minutes with him before rushing back to the office. He was always awake and waiting for her, eyes on the door as soon as he heard the swift clicking of her heels coming down the hallway. For the first few weeks of rehab, their time was filled with my friend narrating the stories of her work at the office, the adventures of her children, the sports scores of her dad's favorite teams, whatever she thought might be of interest to him. He would nod and try to smile, never taking his eyes off her.

After a few weeks of physical therapy, he began to learn how to speak again in faltering, garbled words. He tried to speak to her when she came. She would stop him, encouraging him to rest rather than wear himself out trying to talk. His efforts increased, however, and he eventually managed to sit up when she walked in, smiling as best he could and speaking as clearly as he could manage: " I wahn . . . I wahn . . ." She would try to guess what he wanted as she surveyed the room, adjusting the blinds, clearing away old flowers, "What, Dad? You want lunch? You want something different to eat? You want to go to the bathroom? You want me to call the nurse?" After a few unsuccessful attempts, the father would lay back as his daughter fussed with his pillows and blankets, gave him his lunch, and gathered up his dirty laundry.

"I'll see you tomorrow, Dad. And I'll bring that music you like so much, OK?"

She became desperate to know what her father was trying to communicate, what need he had that wasn't being met. She asked the nurses and called the doctor, but they all claimed he never indicated anything similar to them, leaving her in even greater anguish.

The next week, her dad was sitting upright in a chair when she arrived. She came in, breathless as usual, looked around and said, "Where's your food? I'll call down to the kitchen and see what happened."

He started, "I wahn oo . . ."

"What, Dad? You want to what?"

"I wahn oo . . ."

"You want to what? You want to go for a ride? You want to listen to your music?"

He shook his head.

"I brought your mail. You want me to read to you?"

Again, no.

"The TV? Do you want the TV on?"

No.

More forcefully now, "I. Wahn. Oo."

The daughter became frustrated to the point of tears. "I don't know what you want, Dad. I'm so sorry. Can you show me? Can you please just show me? Look at the thing you want and I'll try harder to get it right."

He didn't take his eyes off her.

"Dad, please. I know there's something you've been trying to tell me for weeks now. I know you need something and you keep asking me for it. Please, help me understand."

With extreme effort, he lifted his left hand and pointed at her. *"I want you."*

"You want me?"

"I. Want. You."

Her father smiled broadly, relieved, and slumped back, dropping his arm. She approached him, fell to her knees in front of him, and melted into a long tear-filled hug. "All this time, that's all you wanted? Me?"

"*You.*"

Her visits continued during the lunch hour. She still arrived breathless and she still rushed out. But she stopped fussing and fretting. She stopped worrying about his pillows and his dishes and the mail and the flowers. She stopped worrying about having everything "just so" and making sure he was happy. She realized that all he ever needed—wanted—was her presence. Her attentiveness. Her reverence.

We fret. Oh, how we fret. Like Martha, we aren't usually fretting over bad things. Food needs to be cooked, houses need to be cleaned, guests need to be served. But our worrying, when it makes us "anxious and burdened," might just be getting in the way and preventing us from seeing the real need right in front of us.

Jesus arrived at Martha's house needing something, but it was none of the things she was worrying over. She was so certain that she *knew* what he needed that she didn't notice his *actual* need. Jesus showed her plainly: "No, Martha, I will not tell your sister to help you. Look more closely—she's got it right. I need only one thing—you. And Mary needs only one thing—me. What, Martha, do you need?"

This story of Martha and Mary doesn't name any other witnesses to the event. Yet, the story endured—and actually became part of the canon of the Bible! This experience was remembered and retold by someone who would have known what happened and its import. Was that person Jesus? Doubtful. Mary? Maybe. But my bet is on Martha. Anyone who has received a direct comeuppance like the one detailed here is loath to let someone *else* tell the tale, much less the hero(ine) of the story. So, if my guess is correct and Martha is the one who immortalized this experience, wow. Just wow. Why would she have done that? I can just imagine Martha relating this story over and over again (with a side laugh at Mary's tendency to deprioritize the laundry), relating the miracle that cured her blindness to the one thing necessary: the presence of God in our midst.

From Martha:

It happened right there in my home. He had come to us on his way to Jerusalem. I remember, he arrived weary and worn. By himself. He came in and I started fussing. But Mary noticed. She sat down and listened to him. Funny, I didn't think to do that. I was fretting over food and drink and—oh, I don't know what all. But then, like a bolt of lightning, he stopped me in my tracks. He saw me and he stopped me. And then . . . oh, then! I saw him, too. He turned my fussing and fretting into vision. And just like that, my burden was lifted. I stopped worrying about everything else. I saw *him*. Suddenly I knew what I needed to do, because I saw what he needed. He was with us because somehow, we were home for him. We were his home! How could I have missed that? Imagine: Jesus coming to just be with my sister and me? How could I have missed that . . . ?

Would I change anything about that afternoon? I don't think so. I'm a fretter, that's all there is to it. I worry, I fuss, and I try to tend to people's needs. That's not going to change anytime soon. But my sister taught me something valuable that day, and it's a lesson not just for me but for every single person who hears this story: go ahead and fret if you must. But never let it become a judgment of others. Never let it blind you to the opportunity and people right in front of you. Never let it blind you to the one thing necessary—God's very presence in your midst.

Chapter 5: John the Baptist
Befriending Doubt: The Gift of Choice

John the Baptist in prison

> When John heard in prison of the works of the Messiah, he sent his disciples to him with this question, "Are you the one who is to come, or should we look for another?" Jesus said to them in reply, "Go and tell John what you hear and see: the blind regain their sight, the lame walk, lepers are cleansed, the deaf hear, the dead are raised, and the poor have the good news proclaimed to them. And blessed is the one who takes no offense at me."
>
> —*Matthew 11:2-6*

I know, I know. Thomas is usually the gospel character associated with doubt. I wonder, though, if every time we speak of "doubting Thomas," John the Baptist smirks a little, realizing he has been let off the hook—again. In this passage from the Gospel of Matthew, it sure seems like John is questioning who Jesus is, apparently expressing doubt as to whether or not he is "the one to come." If you are a careful reader of the gospels, this may be a bit bewildering. Weren't John and Jesus cousins (Luke 1:36)? Didn't John "leap for joy" in recognition of the presence of Jesus while they were both still in the womb (Luke 1:44)? Hadn't John protested against baptizing Jesus on the belief that Jesus was the one who should be baptizing him (Matt 3:13-14)? So why was he now, only a few chapters later, doubting who Jesus was?

That is the question, isn't it? How can someone who is so strong in faith, someone who has known Jesus his whole life, someone who has dedicated the entirety of his existence to the belief that Jesus is exactly who he says he is—how can such a one, at such a critical moment of his life, have doubts? John the Baptist was one of the very few people in Jesus' life who knew who Jesus was from the beginning, who believed in his mission and led others to believe in it as well, and who went "all in" with a full life commitment (see Mark 1:6-8).

As I write this, it is the summer solstice here in the northern hemisphere. Coinciding almost perfectly with this date is the liturgical celebration of the birth of John the Baptist on June 24, exactly six months prior to the birth of Jesus. It is neither accident nor fluke that the feast of John, who proclaimed "He must increase; I must decrease" (John 3:30), is poised right as our entire world teeters on the border of light and dark. As we begin our descent into increasing darkness, we remember the witness of John the Baptist's life: "A man named John was sent from God. He came for testimony, to testify to the light so that all might believe through him. He was not the light, but came to testify to the light. The true light, which enlightens everyone, was coming into the world" (John 1:6-9). That light, Jesus Christ, was born in late December, at the same time as the winter solstice, thus initiating the incremental increase of daylight. "The light shines in the darkness, and the darkness has not overcome it" (John 1:5).[1]

From the beginning, then, even the very heavens confirmed that Jesus was the one who is to come. Additionally, all four gospels attest that at Jesus' baptism, John witnessed the heavens opening up and the Spirit of God descending upon Jesus in dramatic fashion (Mark 1:10-11; Matt 3:16-17; Luke 3:21-22; John 1:32-34).

So how had John seemingly forgotten all of this later in life? What exactly was the quality of the question John raised from prison? *"Are you the one who is to come or should we look for another?"* Was this full-on doubt, a request for confirmation from Jesus, or something else entirely? Was John sending his followers to ask a question *he* had or was he giving them an

---

[1] The symbolism of light and dark expressed here are the experience of the northern hemisphere, wherein Israel, the birthplace of both John and Jesus, is situated.

opportunity to hear directly from Jesus' the answer to a question *they* had?[2]

For now, let's imagine it really was John's question—the same John who "leapt," the same John who witnessed, the same John who sent his own disciples to follow Jesus. To that John, I have questions of my own: Did your faith and doubt happen at the same time? Where did the doubt start—was it disappointment . . . or fear . . . or pride . . . or loss? How did you overcome the doubt and return to your faith in Jesus? Oh boy, do I have questions. How exactly does a person of faith learn to ward off doubt?

My nephew Jeremy has autism spectrum disorder,[3] and one afternoon when he was four years old, I was sitting with him on the living room floor as he worked on a puzzle. It was one of those big-piece puzzles with knobs in the middle of each piece for ease of grabbing. He turned the frame upside down so the dozen or so pieces tumbled onto the carpet, and then, as he placed the empty frame directly in front of him, he started to whimper.

"I can't do it."

I reached for a piece to help him. He slapped my hand away.

"I can't do it," he repeated as he picked up a puzzle piece and put it into its proper place.

I tried to hand him another piece of the puzzle, but he ignored me and grabbed the one that belonged adjacent to the piece he had already placed.

"I can't do it," the mantra continued, but this time he stole a sideways look at me, warning me not to interfere any further.

---

[2] The text is ambiguous. John sends the disciples with a question, but *whose* question it is remains unstated and unimplied.

[3] A misnomer, in my opinion, as this guy insists that everything in his world—*every single thing*—be as ordered as possible. Example: when he was still only a toddler, he would climb into the kitchen pantry and alphabetize the canned goods.

Within two minutes, Jeremy had finished the puzzle while repeatedly insisting that he "couldn't do it." Then, when the last piece was placed, without celebration or ceremony, he simply stood up, looked at the thing like it was an adversary bested, and walked away.

When I first sat down, I thought my nephew was expressing doubt in his ability to accomplish a task, but after he got up, I realized he was giving voice to something else. Jeremy doesn't have the ability to verbalize that "something else," so he left me instead with a life-long meditation. He kept repeating, "I can't do it," even while he *was* doing it. Two seemingly incompatible realities were coexisting—his convincing expression of inability and his clear demonstration of ability. What I was hearing and what I was seeing were two completely different things. When I stopped to actually look at what was happening, I could see what was unfolding in front of my eyes. It was not what I was expecting. I had based my response to him on my own expectations rather than on what I *saw* when I looked at Jeremy.

The question, then, is: in any given circumstance, is my expression of doubt (whether in myself, in others, or in God) genuine disbelief, or is it blindness to something that doesn't conform to my expectations?

John the Baptist was in prison and had questions, maybe even doubts, about Jesus. The text starts, "John heard in prison of the works of the Messiah," implying that John still held belief in Jesus as the Messiah. But then he sent his disciples to ask a direct question about whether or not Jesus was the real deal. Doubt and faith, it seems, lived side by side, not unlike light and darkness at the solstice or Jeremy's ability/inability to do a puzzle. And just like light and darkness or demonstrated puzzle ability, it seems that when it comes to doubt and faith, one element is increasing and the other is decreasing.

Jesus received the messengers but instead of answering their question, decided to pose a question back to John: *Take a look, cousin. The deaf hear, the lame walk, the dead live on. Take a good, long look. And then decide what it is you're looking at. What exactly do you see?*

I can cut John some slack on this one. After all, the long-awaited Messiah foretold by the prophets would come "with vindication, with divine recompense," to save his people Israel (Isa 35:4). This did not exactly seem a good description of what Jesus was doing. Enter stage left: *doubt.* Or, more aptly, the *choice* to doubt.

But then Jesus' reply was a reminder of what comes next in the prophecy: "Then the eyes of the blind shall see, and the ears of the deaf be opened; then the lame shall leap like a stag and the mute tongue sing for joy" (Isa 35:5-6). Or, put a different way, "you have a choice to doubt that I am actually the person you think I am, or to believe—even when things don't look exactly the way you thought they would."

It's as if Jesus is saying: *Yes, you have faith, and it seems you also have some doubts. The real question is: which is increasing and which is decreasing?*

One night, having ordered curbside at a local restaurant, I went with a friend to pick it up at our allotted 6:30 time. We arrived a few minutes early and chatted in the car. When the clock blinked 6:30, I worried out loud that they'd be late. My friend gently said, "Give them the full minute," and sure enough, pretty soon, out came a bouncy teenager with bags in hand. As I pulled away, I noticed the clock change to 6:31. I had *chosen* to question, for no apparent reason other than things didn't show up on the timeframe I wanted (early), even though they showed up on the timeframe promised (right on time).

So here's what I have to say to the Baptizer about Jesus, the chosen one of God: *Give him the full minute, John.*

Sure, Jesus might not look very messianic as he tends to the lepers and hangs out with sinners. He might not look like the kind of messiah you were expecting, brother. But look again. What you have been promised—what *we* have been promised—is right in front of us, doing *exactly* the kind of thing

God promised the messiah would be doing. The evidence before us is clear: *this is Jesus, the one we have known, the one we have believed in, the one who makes the blind see and the deaf hear.* Can I believe in *this kind* of a messiah? It is not so much about what is true and what is false—it is about what I let prevail. Will I let doubt supersede faith or will I choose to let faith hush doubt? What will increase in me and what will decrease?

This is not at all easy—certainly no easier now than it was in John's time. God doesn't always respond to our needs in the ways we expect or hope for, but does God's response cause me to grow in faith or in doubt?

Here's a recent example from my own experience. During the initial weeks of the COVID lockdown, I would go for long walks through my neighborhood and nearby parks, enjoying the fresh air, reveling in the spring flowers, and having long talks with God about some pretty significant issues I was trying to work out. As I walked and thought and prayed through those weeks, I started to notice that I was finding stray coins every single day. Sometimes it was just a tossed nickel on the sidewalk, sometimes a few pennies dropped outside a store, and occasionally a bright shiny quarter. I came to rely on those coins, reading them as signs of God's Providence, small tokens of reassurance that God was with me. My walks were long and it seemed that just when I wasn't expecting it or right when I was considering something of great import, there was my coin. I played with the phenomenon, purposely traversing the exact same route for days at a time, testing God's faithfulness, certain that "today" would be the day I would come home empty-handed. But no, each day brought new coins, new assurances, and the exact same promise: *I am right here; I am with you.*

On one of those walks in the spring of 2020, I came across a dime. I had just been ruminating on a difficult decision, so I picked it up and just looked at it in the palm of my hand for a moment. This time, though, instead of being grateful, I put out a challenge: "OK, God. You know what I'm going through, you know what I need. You tell me you're with me, well, you also promised the hundredfold to those who trust you (Matt 13:23). So if you're for real, send it right now. Send me ten bucks."

What in the world?

How did I so quickly move out of gratitude for a gift freely given to an outright demand of proof? Even when I had a clear-as-day gift of grace sitting right there in the palm of my hand, bolstering my faith, I chose doubt. *What if I'm wrong? What if I'm deluding myself and this isn't God but just some dumb coincidence? What if I'm nothing more than a stupid fool for thinking these are signs from God? What if none of what I believe is true?* I was on a runaway train of doubt, and I let it pick up speed. I *chose* to stay on that train rather than look at the very real confirmation before me, actually *seeing* what I was looking at.

Isn't this so often the case? Whether it's God's faithfulness I'm questioning or the love of someone close to me, even when I have direct proof right in front of my face, clear evidence of something true and beautiful and good, doubt will cast its stormy clouds and obscure what I have long professed to believe. Right when I need the power of my faith the most, doubt creeps in and contorts confidence into question. And in those moments, I forget that I have a choice. The doubts and questions feel more real than the truth, and it's as if I'm at their mercy. The darkness seems to gain victory because I forget that *I can choose light.* I can *choose* to believe in goodness and truth and beauty even when they're not perfect, even when they don't quite look like I was expecting. I can choose to look and see the goodness right in my midst.

I knew I was being ridiculous as I stood there on the sidewalk, throwing that gauntlet down to God. I expected disappointment—I was actually setting the stage for it. I had absolutely no expectation that I would find another coin, much less a ten-dollar bill. All the awe and wonder of the first days of discovery had morphed into the belief that "it'll never happen." I wasn't only choosing doubt, I was convincing myself that there was no other option, that faith was a setup.

Examining the experience now in hindsight, the choice I had is so clear to me. So often in my life, God confirms my faith and provides grace upon grace upon grace, yet I still succumb to doubting God's love, providence, and mercy.

What is up with that?

John the Baptist's reply: "Well, I'm not sure I have the answer to that, but I'll tell you this much: *he must increase; you must decrease.* Keep looking at what you're looking at when you have doubts. And then, choose what you will see."

Well, John, this is what I see: I see a dime in my hand and I see that it's not a ten-dollar bill. *Doubt.*

Or . . . I see this dime in my hand and recognize it as a freely given gift of love from One who has promised never to leave me abandoned. *Faith.*

It is a choice; it is always a choice. What will increase, faith or doubt? Will the light shine in the darkness or will the darkness encroach on the light? Just like John's Messiah, God may not show up in the ways I expect or in the fashion I want, but nevertheless, God will show up.

Let me tell you the end of my "ten bucks" story. I was maybe twenty yards beyond where I had thrown down to God the proverbial "hundredfold gauntlet" when, I kid you not, I came upon a wadded-up bill right off the curb. I stopped dead in my tracks, looked all around me to find the person who must have dropped it, found no one, looked back at my feet, and just gawked at it for a few moments. *Can't be. It just can't be. That's impossible.*

Before I bent over to pick it up, I remember saying out loud, "OK, fine. I hear you, loud and clear. You've got this; you're with me; and no matter what happens, we'll be together, you and me. I hear you—and I believe you." I started to snuffle a little as I leaned down to get it. I let out a gasp of both delight and chagrin as I unfolded a *five*-dollar bill. Leave it to God to give me abundantly more than I needed—but half of what I asked for. (Yes, this is how our relationship works—God is unreasonably patient with my imperfections, inordinately indulgent with my doubts, and very much the jokester. I wouldn't blame you, dear reader, if you have doubts about the truthfulness of this story, but I can provide for you the same evidence that God provided me—a jar full of coins with one crumpled five dollar bill right in the middle.)[4]

I have come to believe that this is the way of faith and doubt. We may never be free of doubts in this lifetime (heck, even John the Baptist had them!), but neither will we be without the freedom to believe. If faith is increasing and doubt is decreasing, something tells me we're on the right track.

From John the Baptist:

I'm not proud of the fact that I had to ask him outright. Maybe I should have known better. Maybe I should have prayed more or listened more, or just straight out had more faith. But there are times, you know? Times when it's just not clear. I was in prison, and for what? For spending my life preparing the way for him, for leading others to him, for believing in him. So yeah, on those dark days, I questioned. I doubted. And I let it get the better of me.

But then the disciples came back and gave me his answer. Oh, so clever. His reference to Isaiah's prophecy was not lost on me and then I knew. I remembered who he was—and it became so much easier to remember who I was. I'm a believer, plain and simple. And he's the one I believe in.

I can't give you faith, friend. You have to choose it for yourself, and that choice unfortunately isn't one and done. Choose it again and again and again . . . with each rising sun.

---

[4] I'm still waiting on the ten.

Chapter 6: Judas
Befriending Betrayal: The Gift of the Whole Truth

The kiss of Judas

One of the Twelve, who was called Judas Iscariot, went to the chief priests and said, "What are you willing to give me if I hand him over to you?" They paid him thirty pieces of silver, and from that time on he looked for an opportunity to hand him over.

When it was evening, [Jesus] reclined at table with the Twelve. And while they were eating, he said, "Amen, I say to you, one of you will betray me." Deeply distressed at this, they began to say to him one after another, "Surely it is not I, Lord?" He said in reply, "He who has dipped his hand into the dish with me is the one who will betray me. The Son of Man indeed goes, as it is written of him, but woe to that man by whom the Son of Man is betrayed. It would be better for that man if he had never been born." Then Judas, his betrayer, said in reply, "Surely it is not I, Rabbi?" He answered, "You have said so."

Judas, one of the Twelve, arrived, accompanied by a large crowd, with swords and clubs, who had come from the chief priests and the elders of the people. His betrayer had arranged a sign with them, saying, "The man I shall kiss is the one; arrest him." Immediately he went over to Jesus and said, "Hail, Rabbi!" and he kissed him. Jesus answered him, "Friend, do what you have come for." Then stepping forward they laid hands on Jesus and arrested him.

Then Judas, his betrayer, seeing that Jesus had been condemned, deeply regretted what he had done. He returned the thirty pieces of silver to the chief priests and elders, saying, "I have sinned in betraying innocent blood." They said, "What is that to us? Look to it yourself." Flinging the money into the temple, he departed and went off and hanged himself.

—Matthew 26:14-16, 20-25, 47-50; 27:3-6

Judas is never an easy fellow to talk about. As a matter of fact, I debated mightily about whether or not to include him in this book. Imagine, then, the difficulty the early Christians—and the other apostles!—experienced as they tried to wrangle with him and what he did in betraying Jesus. The story of Judas appears in all four gospels in varying detail and, as we might suspect, with differing perspectives on his betrayal.[1] All four evangelists agree, however, on the absolute treachery of Judas's choice to betray Jesus Christ. Matthew gives us the most text to examine, as seen above. Luke says little in either his gospel or Acts of the Apostles,[2] only that Satan entered Judas who then conspired with the religious authorities to get Jesus arrested, and ultimately died a terrible death (Luke 22:3-6; Acts 1:16-25). John portrays Judas as possessed by evil and utterly lost (John 6:70;13:27;17:12). Mark seems to be the gentlest of the four gospels, spending little time distinguishing the behavior of Judas from any of the other apostles, including Peter.[3] *That* Judas betrayed Jesus is not in question. That his betrayal led

---

[1] For a simple but close reading of all the scriptural texts referring to Judas Iscariot as well as a broad look at the development of Catholic theology concerning him, I recommend William Kent's "Judas Iscariot," *Catholic Encyclopedia*, vol. 8, which can be accessed online at https://www.newadvent.org/cathen/08539a.htm.

[2] From as early as the second century (St. Irenaeus of Smyrna), Christianity has held that the same author wrote Luke and Acts of the Apostles.

[3] Some detail from Mark is worth considering here, especially since his gospel served as primary source material for Luke and Matthew. In the fourteenth chapter of the Gospel of Mark, none of the apostles come off looking very good. In point of fact, Judas's choices and words are consistently placed alongside the words and choices of the entire group of apostles. For example, immediately prior to the Last Supper, when the woman from Bethany anoints Jesus with costly ointment, Mark tells us "there were some" who became angry and indignant, arguing that the money could have been better spent in providing for the poor (Mark 14:3-5). Only John names Judas as the one who made this complaint "because he was a thief" (John 12:6). Soon after in Mark, when Jesus says during the meal, "One of you will betray me, one who is eating with me," it is quite clear that they are all eating with him. Moreover, each of the Twelve respond to this shocking revelation by asking Jesus if he

to the arrest, torture, and death of Jesus is also inarguable. That the betrayal was reprehensible and indefensible is universally agreed upon (well, except for the Cainite heretics in the second century, but that's a story for another time). What *is* arguable (and thousands of authors and theologians have debated this through the centuries) is the conclusion drawn about Judas's eternal fate as a result of his betrayal.

Betrayal. It's such an ugly word, isn't it? But it's an even uglier reality. Consider for a moment the type of person who comes to mind when you think of betrayal. We might think of famous traitors like Benedict Arnold or the Rosenbergs. Or we may think of different kinds of betrayal like marital infidelity, rumor-spreading by a friend, insider trading. If we are going to reckon with the person of Judas, however, we need to consider more uncomfortable types of betrayals—the personal ones that cut to the bone. Personal betrayal comes in two categories: betrayals I've experienced and betrayals I've committed. Each of these categories can be further examined depending on whether or not forgiveness has occurred. Being forgiven by someone we have betrayed is nothing short of sheer grace. That type of forgiveness creates in the recipient a quiet, hollow space of humility, inviting her to greater wholeness and holiness. Forgiving someone who has betrayed us is a tall order, but it can be done—again, through grace—creating in the giver a tender, vulnerable space of strength and freedom.[4]

---

is talking about them—a response that seems to imply guilty consciences at the very least (Mark 14:18-19).

[4] A word of distinction is needed here. Forgiveness does not ever excuse, justify, or ameliorate bad behavior, especially betrayal. Nor does forgiveness necessarily imply reconciliation. Some circumstances (abuse or addiction, for example) require healing and improved health prior to reconciliation, even if forgiveness has already been given and/or received. For a fuller treatment of my view on this topic, I recommend "I've Been Wronged! Do I Have to 'Turn the Other Cheek,'?" episode 37 of the *Mental Health Matters* podcast from Saint Louis Counseling, available at https://saintlouiscounseling.org/mental-health-matters/ive-been-wronged-do-i-have-to-turn-the-other-cheek/.

Did Jesus forgive Judas? What we know of Jesus is that he *is* forgiveness itself, which makes verse 24 very sobering when Jesus said: "woe to that man by whom the Son of Man is betrayed. It would be better for that man if he had never been born." Never been born? That sure doesn't sound like forgiveness. What is going on here? Is Jesus really saying that his friend's life was a mistake, that his very existence as a person was offensive? That is a difficult perspective to defend in light of the entirety of the gospels. For example, immediately after Judas's act of betrayal, when he greeted Jesus with a kiss (what?!), Jesus still called him "friend." How are we to understand all of this?

Let's read it again: "it would have been better *for that man* . . ." A close reading of the gospel narratives raises many questions about Judas, his motivation, and his state of mind in the last days of Jesus' life. Was turning Jesus over to the authorities an outright act of infidelity? Was Judas hoping to "jump start" a cultural and religious revolution that would reveal Jesus as Messiah? Did he expect things to go differently than they did? Was Jesus' arrest and death sentence a surprise to Judas?

What we know is that after he handed Jesus over to the authorities, Judas regretted his decision, returned the money, and hanged himself. That doesn't sound to me like someone responding to "everything going perfectly according to plan." That sounds a lot like despair to me.

Despair might very well be the most dreadful of all human emotion, for reasons best explained by Søren Kierkegaard: "The despairing individual is simply a negative step further away from the truth, and from salvation."[5] If it is true that Judas despaired as a result of Jesus' condemnation and crucifixion, then his mind and soul were quickly becoming more

---

[5] Søren Kierkegaard, *The Sickness Unto Death* (Princeton, NJ: Princeton University Press, 1980), 44.

and more distant from all things true and good and beautiful. Indeed, Judas's despair led him further away from the love and mercy of Jesus, the one who called himself the Truth (John 14:6).

It is possible that Judas believed that what he had done was unforgiveable, wholly outside the reach of God's mercy. If that is true, though, what falsehood must Judas have believed about God to imagine that he was capable of thwarting God's plan of salvation? To believe in a god like that—a god powerless in the face of our mistakes, a god who can be vanquished by human judgment or choice—narrows life and love immensely. To believe in a god like that is to have failed to really know who Jesus was—or to have failed to truly believe in him.

When I was a freshman in high school, a classmate of mine consistently cracked me up during class. One day, what started as a pun contest turned into a minor ruckus, disrupting the teacher's lecture and making the whole room erupt in laughter. When she turned around from the board, not having heard the joke which I'm sure she would have appreciated, she was fed up, and told me to gather my things and go. She didn't tell me exactly *where* to go, just to go, so I did. I remember standing in the hallway wondering what, exactly, a person was supposed to do upon eviction just ten minutes before the lunch bell. I assumed I should report myself to the principal's office and explain the circumstances, taking nobly the penalty for getting kicked out of class, but instead I just waited it out and headed to the cafeteria. I dreaded what my teacher would do when she found out I hadn't gone to the office. Would I get detention? Would she call my parents? Would I have to transfer into a different class? Would she lower my grade? I hesitantly showed up for class the next day, waiting for the other shoe to drop. When it didn't, I was the epitome of good behavior that day and for the rest of the semester. No real punishment ever resulted, but after being ousted I could not look that teacher in the eye and I avoided interaction with her at all costs. I was humiliated and embarrassed, and I just knew that every time she saw me she thought, "That girl—she's a troublemaker. I wish she had never been in my class."

I kept this belief for the entirety of high school, this belief in a teacher who was so negatively affected by my antics and who resented me for it. For the next three and a half years, I was afraid that she would call me out at any moment, terrified of what she had said about me to other faculty members. The power this "intimidating, bitter teacher" had over me was strong. Finally, right before graduation when I knew I had nothing to lose, I approached her to give a full apology for both my behavior in her freshman class and also my avoidance of the just punishment I had coming to me. Truth be told, I just wanted to be out from under her spell. I timidly poked my head into her classroom one afternoon and asked if I could speak with her.

"Of course! What can I do for you, Virginia?" she asked.

Ah, a façade of kindness. Not what I was expecting. No matter— full speed ahead.

"Well, uh, I wanted to apologize to you."

"What on earth for?"

"For being disrespectful and disruptive during your class freshman year. When you kicked me out of class, I never went to the office to face the consequences. I just went to the cafeteria. I'm sorry I haven't been honest before now, and I'm really sorry I never apologized to you. I know you must think I'm really sneaky but I promise I'm not and I really did learn my lesson that day."

She looked at me thoughtfully for a moment before cocking her head to one side and saying, "I have a question for you."

"Here it comes," I thought. *"Why did I decide to do this? I was almost scot-free and now she's going to let me have it, and right before graduation!"*

Ever so gently she said, "You're convinced that I define you now—and have always defined you—according to what happened that day. What must you believe about *me* to think that I could harbor that kind of resentment against a student?"

Stunned, all I could say was, "What do you mean?"

"Virginia, you were fourteen. Believe me, I'm used to teaching fourteen-year-olds. Nothing much surprises or disturbs me. I was probably having a bad day and had just reached the end of my rope. I can't even picture the scene you're describing, much less remember the details, but I can tell you this: I imagine I fully expected that you would just go to lunch. You need to know something now, though. I have not been nursing negative thoughts about you all these years. That is not at all consistent with who I am. What's more, what I know about you is a lot bigger than one incident three years ago. You are much, much more than that fourteen-year-old girl. Now, tell me something: is this the reason you never took any of my other classes?"

"Yeah . . ." I replied, suddenly regretful.

She sighed a deep sigh. "Wow, I'm so sorry about that. It kind of makes me wish you had been placed in a different section as a freshman. Without that experience, I might have had the chance to get to know the real you—and you might have gotten to know the real me."

Echoes of Kierkegaard: *One negative step further from the truth . . .*

And echoes of Jesus: *It would have been better for that girl if she had never taken that class . . .*

True, my behavior wasn't exactly the death-dealing betrayal of Judas, and I am not trying to compare teenage goofiness to traitorous decisions, but I learned one of the most valuable truths about God, love, and life that day: *each one of us is a lot bigger than our bad behaviors.* When we can't see past those mistakes—either our own or someone else's—we aren't seeing the fullness of reality. We miss getting to know the real person. We miss out on the truth of ourselves, we miss out on the truth of others, and we forget the truth of God.

Judas had some bad behaviors, no two ways about it. So do I. So do you. So do the people who have hurt us, even those who have betrayed us. But no one is defined by their worst choices, even if those choices have disastrous consequences. Maybe in focusing on Judas's betrayal, we are looking in the wrong direction. Maybe the reason he's not given much airtime in the gospels is because the writers knew his treachery would distract us from the actual Truth: *Jesus*.

A popular question from my own theology students has always been, "Did Judas go to hell?" and it always initiates a lively discussion. Perhaps the more appropriate question is, "What do you believe about God?" Let's imagine for a moment that Judas's story didn't end the way Matthew 27:5 indicates, with his suicide. Let's imagine for a moment that Judas fled the scene like the others did, sat in his guilt and shame for three days, and then heard the stories of the empty tomb and the claim that Jesus had risen from the dead. Envision for a moment Judas encountering the risen Christ. What do we imagine would have occurred?[6]

Our answer to this question tells us *exactly* what we believe about God.

Is there any sin, any treachery, any wickedness outside the scope of God's love and forgiveness?

Nope, not according to the Christian gospels.

Is God's love truly unconditional?

Yup.

Is there any sinner, betrayer, or evildoer who cannot receive God's love and forgiveness?

Actually, yes there is: *the one who refuses it*.

God's love and forgiveness are for everyone, period. But not everyone accepts them. I couldn't accept the forgiveness of my high school teacher because I didn't believed it existed.

---

[6] For a beautiful treatment of the question of Judas's salvation, I strongly recommend twentieth-century theologian Hans Urs von Balthasar, *Dare We Hope "That All Men Be Saved"?* (San Francisco: Ignatius Press, 1988).

It did. I didn't believe she was someone who would give me that forgiveness. *She was.* My lack of belief didn't make the forgiveness nonexistent, it just made it inaccessible to me. Not until I was willing, able, and ready to receive could I actually gain the freedom and healing of her forgiveness—and know the truth of who she was.

The Catholic sacrament of reconciliation has four elements: contrition, confession, absolution, penance.[7] Matthew 27:3-4 tells us that Judas deeply regretted his betrayal and confessed his sinfulness to the chief priests and elders. Contrition and confession. Absolution comes next—but Judas pre-empted it. Rather than remembering who Jesus was, Judas focused on his own sin and failure—and despaired. Had he endured the agony of his own betrayal *from the perspective of Jesus*, he may very well have been the main character in one of the gospel accounts of the resurrected Christ.

Was Judas's biggest mistake his betrayal of Jesus? I think not; in my opinion, where Judas went wrong was in looking at himself instead of at Jesus. He seemed to have falsely believed that his betrayal was unforgiveable. He may not have been able to forgive himself for it; the other apostles may not have been able to forgive him for it; but Jesus could and Jesus did. God is a lot bigger than our biggest screwups. The question is whether or not we will accept the forgiveness and mercy given to us. Will we move one step further away from the truth and salvation or one step closer?

Oh, and one other thing: will we, in turn, give that same love and mercy to others?

When we are on the receiving end of someone else's malice or disdain, can we find a way to step back and perceive what might be happening under the surface? When someone is lashing out (verbally, physically, emotionally, psychologically), something is not right in the person, not 100 percent healthy.

---

[7] See *Catechism of the Catholic Church*, articles 1442–70.

This does not *excuse* the behavior, but it sure as heck might explain it. We do not need to endure or accept bad treatment, but we can realize that we have a choice in responding to the person who is displaying it.

For one summer—and one summer only—I was a camp counselor for "rising kindergarteners." (Translation: four-year-olds.) On the playground one day, little Jack was provoking a group of girls who were trying to play a simple game of catch. (Something to know about Jack: he was one of those kids who was always in trouble. At age four, he had already perfected a defiant scowl and "I'm-not-doing-it-I-don't-care-what-you-say" screech, and he knew exactly how to push every single kindergartener's buttons—which he did on a regular basis.) So when the girls came up to me complaining that Jack was bothering them, I asked him to stop and tried to redirect his energies—to no avail. At the third complaint, Jack was given time-out and had to stand by me for five minutes. I must confess that at this time in my life, I had no experience teaching young kids, and so I thought that simply telling him to stand by me would do the trick. When time was up, I looked down to find that Jack was not "standing by me" but had returned to the girls' circle and had begun throwing pebbles at them. I intervened, moved the girls to a safer spot, and addressed the culprit:

"Alright, bud, now you're in time out for the rest of recess *and* you have to hold my hand while you stand here so I know you haven't gone anywhere."

"I don't like you!" Jack growled.

"I don't care!" I maturely countered.

And then, since I chose to look away from him so I could ignore his growly attitude, I did not see that he was gearing up to kick me with all the might his little body could muster.

When the blow landed straight on my shin, my immediate reaction was to double over in pain and grab my leg with my free hand, which brought me eye-to-eye with Jack. He was ready for it. His little face was hardened and prepared for whatever I was going to say to him. He was mad, and now I was, too. Both of us seemed to be thinking, "Bring it!"

To this day, I believe that every guardian angel in heaven came rushing toward me in that moment to manage the words that came out of my mouth, because what I said was not at all what I was thinking but instead a very loud, very strong, "Why did you do that?!"

And then, everything in that little boy crumbled as he said, "My daddy's leaving—and it's all my fault."

Instantaneous change of emotion—for both of us. He started to sob, I forgot about my throbbing shin, and that tiny little body leaned in for a hug from the person who only moments before he had seen as public enemy number one. *One step closer to the truth and salvation.*

When we have the opportunity to learn the story behind someone's bad behavior, we learn a lot. Don't get me wrong, it's no magic wand. Jack continued to get into all kinds of trouble that summer and he still had to face the consequences. But something shifted in that little kid. Every time he was in time-out, he wanted to stand by me and hold my hand. No words necessary, just a simple presence, a simple knowing.

Jack is now close to forty years old and I often find myself wondering if he's still "throwing rocks." Those rocks look and feel a lot different when we're adults—they may take the form of aggression or manipulation or road rage or any variety of abuse—and it becomes a lot harder to blurt the truth out loud to someone, breaking open our hearts with the tears that heal. Bad behavior cannot be tolerated or excused, but maybe, just maybe, it can be put in perspective. Maybe we can zoom out far enough past the immediate experience to see that it is just one piece of a person's whole story.

Jack is much more than a stone thrower; I am much more than a disruptive student; Judas was much more than a betrayer. The truth is, he was an apostle. He was a believer.

He was a friend. In the big picture, he was also the beloved of God. I hope and pray that in the end, he claimed it.

From Judas:

> Learn from me—please learn from me. I was so wrong in so many ways. My life could have been so different if I had only opened myself up to believing that everything Jesus said and did was true—and true *for me*. Sure, I preached it to others—I was on fire with his message of love and healing and tenderness and mercy. I preached it pretty eloquently, actually. The problem was, I never quite believed it was true for me, too. I always knew Jesus and the Father loved unconditionally, forgave sinners, welcomed the lost, healed the sick. I just believed that if they knew how bad I was, how sinful, how lost, how sick . . . well, it would be too much. They would be horrified. Heck, I was horrified at myself. And the others were pretty horrified, too. So how could God not be?
>
> Well, here's how. God is not us. God is not just a bigger, better version of us. God is God, and God is love. Read it again, friends: God is Love. Unconditional, unmerited, unstoppable love. It's hard to accept, I get it. Believe me, I *really* get it. It is hard to accept, but you know what's harder? Not accepting it.
>
> Live, friends. Live in the Love that is yours. It'll change your life.

Chapter 7: Mary

Befriending Anguish: The Gift of Pondering

Pietà

> Standing near the cross of Jesus were his mother and his mother's sister, Mary the wife of Clopas,[1] and Mary Magdalene. When Jesus saw his mother and the disciple whom he loved standing beside her, he said to his mother, "Woman, behold, your son." Then he said to the disciple, "Behold, your mother." And from that hour the disciple took her into his home.
>
> —*John 19:25-27*

※

Since Mary shows up so frequently in the gospels, any number of her characteristics could have been selected for this chapter. I am choosing this final mention of her in the Gospel of John for one specific reason, and it is the first word of the passage: *standing*.

What was Mary doing in this scene? She was standing. This might seem unremarkable since Mary obviously did many things in her lifetime—she stood, she sat, she walked, she cried, she spoke. So why single out this description of *standing*? Contextually, we know that she wasn't standing just anywhere, she was standing at the foot of the cross. Two thousand years later this language is commonplace, but let's remember that

---

[1] Christian and Orthodox traditions have long held that Clopas, mentioned here, and Cleopas, mentioned in chapter 9 of this book from the walk to Emmaus, are likely one and the same person. Testaments from the early Christian chronicler Hegesippus the Nazarene (ca. 110–180 CE) and Eusebius of Caesarea (ca. 260–339 CE) propose that Clopas/Cleopas/Cleophas was brother to Joseph, making "Mary the wife of Clopas" the sister-in-law of Mary, mother of Jesus. The three Marys in this passage, then, would be Mary (mother of Jesus), Mary (sister-in-law to Mary), and Mary Magdalene. For a fuller treatment of this background and history, I recommend Richard Bauckham's "The Relatives of Jesus," *Themelios* 21 (1996), available at http://tgc-documents.s3.amazonaws.com/themelios/Themelios21.2.pdf.

this particular location was the place of an execution and, more poignantly, the execution of her son. Jesus had been put to death by the Romans under the Jewish accusation of blasphemy, the supreme offense of reviling God. Jewish law regarding such a crime required that "a sinner of this kind should be killed in the most awesome way, by being hanged on a tree before his people (whom he has betrayed) and before God (whom he has blasphemed). And while he is hanging on the tree he is, according to the word of the Torah, accursed by God and men."[2] For a Jewish mother to be present at such a scene would indicate that she believed her son to be innocent, which we know Mary did. (Had she believed her son to be guilty, she would never have shown up at his execution, since her faithfulness to God would supersede her dedication to her child.) But if a first-century Jewish woman believed her son innocent of the crime for which he was being killed, the expected response would be wailing, invoking God's wrath upon the executioners, or protesting the injustice incurred, as demonstrated by her Hebrew forebears.[3] Mary did none of this. Instead, she stood, silent and still.

What Mary gave to Jesus in that moment was genuine presence. As he hung on the cross, breathing his last, rejected by the crowds, abandoned by his apostles, scorned by the religious leaders, and feeling forsaken by his heavenly Father, whom did his eyes fall upon? His mother. He saw her standing with him, attentive, prayerful, trusting, *faithful*. What Mary gave to her son in his last agonizing moments was the assurance that he was not alone. She was *there* as mother, disciple,

---

[2] Torleif Elgvin, "The Messiah Who Was Cursed on the Tree," *Themelios* 22 (1997): 15.

[3] Consider Rizpah's vigil over her sons' bodies after David handed them over to be killed (2 Sam 21:1-14), Tamar's bold challenge of the patriarch Judah for the benefit of her unborn sons (Gen 38), and Esther's risky appeal to the king on behalf of the Jewish people who had refused to practice idolatry (Esther 4, C, D).

and faithful believer. Jesus saw her and knew that she had remained with him—to the end. She could not alleviate his physical suffering but she would not add to his emotional or moral suffering by revealing her own anguish to him. She chose to do nothing beyond what he was doing: accepting what God was allowing to happen. She simply stood—in silent witness to him and all that he was, all that he would always be. And to the promises of God.

Hearken back for a moment to the annunciation, when the angel Gabriel appeared to Mary as a young girl (likely only about fourteen years old) telling her of God's plan that she would bear the Son of God for the salvation of the world. What was her response? *"Fiat."*[4] *Let it be done to me according to your word* (Luke 1:38). Some thirty years later on that hill of crucifixion, Mary's prayer seemed to be the same, but this time uttered as silent witness at the foot of the cross. *Let it be done to me—to you—to us—according to God's word.*

Wait, hold up for a second. She said *what*?

Forgive me for a moment while I digress. Even on my best spiritual and personal days—on days when my faith is strong and my hope is soaring and my trust and commitment are at their peak—even on those days, I struggle to utter the simple prayer of *fiat*, "let it be done." I have had great times with God (as I imagine you have as well), times when I was ready for anything God would do or ask, times when I was generous and grateful and open. In those times, my prayer—my *best* prayer, mind you—is usually something along the lines of, "Yes, God, I believe. Yes, I trust in you. Thy will be done. Just tell me what you need me to do and I'll do it. Show me where you want me to be and I'll go. Say what you want me to know and I'll follow." That's a pretty darned good prayer, if I do say so myself. But it doesn't hold a candle to Mary's prayer.

---

[4] The single Latin word "fiat" is the third person singular present subjunctive case of the verb *fieri*, to become, and is best translated "let it be done."

Mary prays, "*Fiat.*" She doesn't say, "Tell me what you need me to do. I'll follow, I'll trust, I'll go, I'll do it." No, she says, "Let it be done *to* me according to *your* word." Notice the difference? In my prayer, where is the initiative? Who is the primary agent of action? What is the focus? Me, me, me. Even if well-intentioned, I must admit there is still a pretty strong sense of ego involved—or at least a desire for some measure of control.

In Mary's prayer, where is the initiative, who is controlling, what is the focus? God, God, God. No ego, no grasping for control. Hers is a prayer of utter surrender to the action of God. She doesn't promise the faithfulness of her own service, she promises faithfulness to the agency of God. This is a much harder prayer in my opinion, requiring the conversion of my well-intentioned, "let me do it for you, God" to a much more humble, much more vulnerable, "let it be done *by you*, God, and I'll show up."

I'll show up in witness to you, in witness to all that you are doing in and around and through me. I'll show up believing. I'll show up trusting. *I'll show up.* This prayer is a letting go, a freefall into the mystery of true faith. This is a prayer exemplified not only by Mary's *"fiat"* at the annunciation, but also by her stance at the foot of the cross: Mary stood.

Let it be done according to God's word.

Even if God's word is silence.

Jesus hung on the cross just hours after having pleaded in the Garden of Gethsemane for the Father to spare him the "cup" of all that was to come on Good Friday (Matt 26:39; Luke 22:42). And then Good Friday happened in all its horror. The Father did not spare his Son the agony, the mockery, the desertion, the torture, or the cross. Moreover, in the last hours of his earthly life, Jesus prayed from the cross in what seemed tormented lament, expressing the anguish of being abandoned by God. This God-forsakenness was yet one more suffering added to the physical agony, possibly even more bitter to swallow than the gall put to his lips—and Jesus' outcry received no perceptible response from the Father whatsoever (see Mark 15:23-34, Matt 27:33-46).

And Mary stood.

Let it be done according to your word. You, my beloved son, are not protesting. The Father is not intervening. You are both allowing this, all of it: undergoing unspeakable pain and suffering, abandonment, crucifixion, death. Father and Son are both letting this be, so what am I to do? I want this to stop, I want it to be different, yet they are not stopping this, not changing it. They are accepting and allowing . . . all of it. So how can I do anything else, want anything else? Wouldn't that be a betrayal of you, my son, and all you are, all that you have come to give? You are accepting all, enduring all, forgiving all. My choice, my witness, my companionship, can be no different. If you are not protesting, neither can I. But I will remain with you, I will remain present, faithful, trusting. You were chosen for all, you are open to all, you are faithful through all. So must I be. Let it be done. I am here.

Just as Mary asked the angel Gabriel, "How is this to be?" at the annunciation, I imagine her at the foot of the cross, turning over in her heart all that led up to that moment and wondering, "How is *this* the fulfillment of his mission? How is my son's cruel death the will of the Father? How is this to be?" Although Scripture doesn't record it, I imagine Mary pondered all these questions and happenings in her heart, just as she had from the very beginning (see Luke 2:19, 51).

I once heard a fascinating commentary on Michaelangelo's *Pietà*, the famous Renaissance sculpture at Saint Peter's Basilica in Rome. This piece was the first of his three depictions of Mary holding the dead body of Jesus after he was taken down from the cross. During his lifetime, Michaelangelo defended the fact that the figures of Jesus and Mary are not proportional. Mary's body is significantly larger than the adult Jesus' corpse, and he is draped across her lap in such a way that holding him in the manner portrayed would not be possible. Her countenance is youthful and serene as she gazes downward, focused not on Jesus' face, but apparently absorbed in silent, somber reflection. Her right hand cradles Jesus across his shoulder blades, seeming to envelope him in her robes—or his?—and her left hand is outstretched, palm up, in a posture of offering or prayer. The commentary I heard theorized that perhaps in his rendering of this particular *Pietà*, Michaelangelo was not intending to represent the moment of Christ's death, but rather of his birth.

Mary, cradling her son; Mary, pondering all that had occurred; Mary, wondering about what was yet to come; Mary, reflecting on how she might best remain faithful to all that God was doing in, through, and around her; Mary, assenting to all; Mary, praying, *"Let it be done."*

Is this a description of Mary at Christ's birth after the annunciation or at his death after the crucifixion? Or both?

In some ways, birth and death can be considered the same point on the circle of life. What we experience as human birth is a death to the safe haven of the womb where we have been cared for by a yet-unknown, yet-unseen mother. What we experience as human death is a rebirth into a new form of life, *eternal* life. We leave the familiar experience of temporality where we have made a home, and abandon ourselves to a yet-unknown, yet-unseen future.

When I taught Catholic theology, I would often make use of the following story to offer the students a way of thinking about death, by way of analogy to birth:

Once upon a time, there were twin babies in the womb talking about what would happen when they were born. The younger one asked, "Do you believe in life after birth?"

The older twin replied, "No, I don't."

The younger continued, "Do you believe in the existence of a Mother?"

The older twin replied, "No. Believing in 'Mother' is just a way people cope with the fact that when we're born, that's the end. It's a fanciful idea with absolutely no proof behind it. If Mother is real, then where is she? How come I can't see her or talk to her or reach out and touch her hand like I can yours?"

The younger twin countered, "But who has provided all that we have here? Who is holding it all together, taking care of us? Mustn't there be some explanation for how we are fed, how we have this safe, cozy place to live and grow and be?"

"Explanation? Sure, there's an explanation, but it's not 'Mother.' We live in a womb, and one day that womb will contract to birth us away, the way every womb has contracted for every baby all throughout time. At that point, we will be deprived of daily nourishment, protection, and access to life. Even if 'the other side' of birth is real, we would be too small and feeble to survive anywhere else. Don't be frightened by that reality, it'll be OK. It just reminds us to enjoy all that we have here and now. Gratitude is the key."

"Gratitude, yes. But . . . sometimes, when we're real quiet and there's no other noise around, can't you hear her singing? I just know there's a Mother out there waiting for us to be born. I just know it. And I feel like she knows us already, that she has a special name selected for us, that she's preparing a place for us, that we belong to her and she to us. Don't you think so?"

"I'd *like* to think so, but there's no evidence for that belief. You hear singing, I hear the swish of amniotic fluid. Who's right? Only time will tell. But what I do know is this, when we are born, we are going to go through a very dark, narrow passageway—and it will be painful. It sounds scary, but it's perfectly natural and there's no way around it. But I'm afraid there's nothing on the other side."

"Yes, that's scary. Darkness and pain aren't exactly great things to look forward to, but I still think there will be something on the other side. I *believe* there is even if I can't prove it. I believe Mother is real and I believe that when we are born, we will see her face-to-face and somehow come to know ourselves better in the process, as an image of her. And when it is time for us to be born, I am convinced—just *convinced*—that we will experience life after birth."

"Only time will tell," said the older twin.

Christianity teaches that birth and death are but two sides of the same coin of life—one starting our earthly life, the other ushering in our eternal life. This belief is founded on the resurrection of Jesus from the dead, a reality that his mother Mary had not yet experienced when the body of her crucified son was placed in her arms at the foot of the cross. Did she believe in life after death? We don't know. But we *do* know that she believed in the power of God to do more than what we could ever imagine possible. She had good reason to believe—she had already experienced it. The human heart can only long for something it has already experienced to some degree. Mary's longing for what God *could* do through the death of Jesus was borne from her experience of what God had *already* done in her life and in her son's.

The question of faith is a tricky one. I tend to think it's not so much a "seeing is believing" reality, as it is "believing is seeing." In my experience, when I have waited for God to show up or prove something, I have often been disappointed. When I have become quiet instead and looked around to notice where God had *already* showed up, I was able to see more than I could have ever believed possible.

My sister and brother-in-law Anne and Mike collect coins just like I do. Well, that's not completely true. They don't "collect" them, exactly. They find them. *Lots* of them. Each time Anne or Mike finds a penny, they deposit it in a container reserved for a particular prayer intention. They have little mason jars all around the house filled with coins, and can tell you what each one represents: one for baby Maya's surgery, one for Rachel's pregnancy, and so on. Some see this as superstitious or trite. Others see it as goofy or even delusional. Not me. I see it as proof of their faith that when we believe in the care of God for his loved ones, we will find promises everywhere that our faith is not in vain.

Anne and Mike don't go out looking for coins. They go out *praying for people*. And time and time again, they come home with a dime and a penny to put in the prayer jar. Believing is seeing. Or, as Jesus said, "Seek and you will find" (Matt 7:7).

Seeking evidence of God's presence may very well keep us peering into the shadows of the night, attuned to every perceived threat, and fearful beyond measure that we might not survive the night. But *praying* in the dark, keeping vigil for what we *believe must come*, will sustain us through the bleakest hours, all the way up until the first rays of dawn appear and the morning star rises in our hearts (2 Pet 1:19).

Mary endured the darkest hours of Good Friday. The dawn that appeared on Holy Saturday was far from a joyous star rising in her heart. The light of *that* day did not illuminate a world rejoicing in beauty and hope, but only a world bereft of her son. How did she endure the anguish of his absence? Scripture doesn't tell us, but it was likely the same way she endured every other sorrow: by continuing to keep vigil for the dawn she knew *must come*—even if it hadn't arrived yet.

In his *Spiritual Exercises*, St. Ignatius of Loyola offers an invitation to pray imaginatively about the risen Jesus appearing to his mother Mary. Ignatius encourages a creative prayer experience to visualize the reunion between mother and son in that Holy Saturday waiting time.[5] Because a key tenet of Ignatian spirituality is generosity in the use of imagination,

---

[5] The *Spiritual Exercises* is essentially a guidebook for spiritual directors who lead retreatants through an extended experience of meditation and contemplation. The use of imagination in the *Exercises* is critical, inviting the retreatant to explore spiritual possibility and engage in dialogical encounter with God, self, and others. Therefore, although there is no scriptural reference to the resurrected Jesus appearing to his mother Mary, Ignatius encourages this reflection as an opportunity for retreatants to deepen and personalize their own experience of the risen Jesus.

I have never had any trouble envisioning this scene. I picture Mary sitting quietly at home on that Sabbath day after having witnessed the murder of her son the day before. I picture her pondering, remembering, praying. I imagine her doing what she had spent her entire life doing—recalling what God had already done and wondering what God was currently doing, believing that there was more to the story than what met the eye. I imagine her being very still, very quiet. And then, I imagine the risen Jesus showing up. I picture Mary looking up at him, smiling, gently nodding, and saying, "Ahhhhh, so *that's* it."

"Yeah, ma, that's it."

"It was death you had to defeat, huh?"

"Seems so."

"Well done, son. Well done."

"Did you know, ma?"

"Know what?"

"That it was going to go like this? That I'd be back?"

"Not exactly. I knew there was more to come. I knew your mission wasn't finished with that awful cross. I knew Love would win. It always does."

"Thank you."

"For what?"

"For staying with me. For being there. For showing up. For believing—all the way through."

"That's what mothers do."

"No, ma. You're more than that. You're so much more. Remember what I told you yesterday? To take care of John and let him take care of you?"

"Yes."

"Here's what I meant. You still have work to do. I no longer need your mothering the way I have up to now, but others will. They *all* will. I give you to them. And I give them to you. You belong to them now—just like they belong to me. Nothing can change that belonging anymore; nothing will separate them from my love—not anguish, distress, persecution, peril, violence; neither death nor life, nor present things, nor future things, nor height, nor depth, nor *any other thing* will *ever* separate them from the love of God come through me. For in all these things, we have conquered overwhelmingly." (See Romans 8:35-39.)

And Mary said, "Let it be done, son. Always and everywhere—*let it be done.*"

From Mary:

Don't be afraid. I know it sounds like a lot, the surrender and the *fiat*. But don't be afraid. That's what the angel said to me, and it's all I ever needed. Because as soon as I was able to say, "Let it be done," from that point forward, you know what? God was with me. *Literally!*

The same is true for you. It is all true—it really is all true. I know it's hard to trust, scary to believe. But you can do hard things, and his love is so much bigger than your fear.

You're not alone. He is with you—and I'm here, too. You are never ever alone. When it feels like it, just take a moment to sit quietly like I did on Holy Saturday. You might just find that in those darkest hours before the sun rises, the Son already rose.

Chapter 8: Longinus

Befriending Error:
The Gift of Conversion

St. Longinus, martyr

> Jesus said, "It is finished." And bowing his head, he handed over the spirit.
> Now since it was preparation day, in order that the bodies might not remain on the cross on the sabbath, for the sabbath day of that week was a solemn one, the Jews asked Pilate that their legs be broken and they be taken down. So the soldiers came and broke the legs of the first and then of the other one who was crucified with Jesus. But when they came to Jesus and saw that he was already dead, they did not break his legs, but one soldier thrust his lance into his side, and immediately blood and water flowed out. An eyewitness has testified, and his testimony is true; he knows that he is speaking the truth, so that you also may [come to] believe.
>
> —*John 19:30-35*

Some things are just hard to say. One phrase in particular proves exceedingly difficult for many people: "I was wrong." An admission of, "Oh wow, I was 100 percent off-base on that one," is pretty tough for most people. Many years ago when I was living in New York City, I had spent an enjoyable Sunday afternoon at the making of a sci-fi movie in Lower Manhattan. The city had cordoned off several streets in order to record a scene from what would later become the 1998 film release *Godzilla*. It was fascinating to observe scenes of hysteria and destruction without, obviously, having an actual monster for the cast to see or hear. A loud, high-pitched siren controlled by the crew indicated that Godzilla was stomping his foot as he ambled down the street, so with each screech of the siren, the actors would flinch and fall as if a mini-earthquake had occurred—with some groupings appearing to get squished along the way. It was absolutely fascinating. When I was relating the experience to my housemate over pizza that night, I laughed about how silly the premise of the story was, saying, "Isn't it crazy to think a multi-million dollar enterprise is based on the idea of a giant lizard attacking New York?"

She said, matter-of-factly, "Godzilla isn't a lizard. It's a gorilla."

I flippantly countered, "No, you're thinking of King Kong. Godzilla's a huge dinosaur-like reptile thing."

To my surprise, she dug her heels in. "No, *you're* wrong. Godzilla is an ape. That's why it's called Godzilla. Godzilla, gorilla. See?"

Somewhat taken aback by both her error and her conviction of its accuracy, I immediately realized that nothing I said would change her mind, so I decided to stand down. I figured, rather than ruin an otherwise delightful evening, I would revisit the question some other time after I could gather more evidence. (This was long before the existence of Siri or Alexa, the easy argument-settlers for such situations.)[1] To defuse the situation, I changed the subject.

"Oh look, it's time for the evening news. Mind if I flip it on while we eat?"

"Sure, go ahead."

One of the closing news stories that night, serendipitously, was the filming of *Godzilla* in Lower Manhattan. As the anchors described the disruption of traffic and the timeline for production, they showed an image from the original 1954 film, and there it was, in vibrant technicolor: a giant lizard ravaging the city.

I turned smugly to see what my friend's reaction was, ready to revel in the "I told you so" moment. She kept her gaze fixed straight ahead and I thought she wasn't going to say anything. Then, without taking her eyes off the screen, she simply said, "How about that?"

---

[1] If you want a hearty laugh, ask Siri if Godzilla is a lizard.

Knowing her as I do, I recognized this simple utterance as her admission of fault, so I simply snorted and said, "Yeah, how about that? Funny looking monkey, don't you think?"

And we laughed our fool heads off.

That was the day I learned that sometimes the universe really does right itself without my help. It was also the day I came to understand that when we believe something to be true and are utterly convinced that we are in the right, it is really, *really* hard to conceive that we might be wrong. Everything in our world seems to reinforce our erroneous conclusions—the media we consume, the company we keep, even the religion we profess.[2] Once we are proven wrong, however, it takes quite a bit of humility, courage, and plain old backbone to say out loud, "Well heck. I got that all-the-way wrong." Instead, our instinct (or mine, at least) is to defend, explain, argue, or justify, when really, a simple admission of error would be much more appropriate—not to mention more constructive. Admitting our mistakes is the first step to experiencing true conversion of heart, and it is an essential building block for loving relationships. In my opinion, no Scripture passage demonstrates this more eloquently than the one from John 19 that opens this chapter.

I did not realize that the soldier at the foot of the cross had a name until I visited Saint Peter's Basilica in Rome. There, right next to the papal altar, I happened upon Bernini's statue of St. Longinus.[3] *"Who's that?"* I wondered. *"Surely he must be someone of great significance in the early church since his image depicts such a faith-filled individual, cruciform in stance* (to depict discipleship to Jesus Christ) *and holding a staff. Wait, no, that's*

---

[2] Consider the Crusades, the Salem witch trials, or the early Christian defense of slaveholding, to name just a few of the more sobering examples.

[3] To see the statue as well as its location in the basilica and historical relevance, visit https://stpetersbasilica.info/Statues/StLonginus/StLonginus.htm.

not a staff. It's a spear. Saint Sebastian? No, it says 'Longinus.' Who the heck is that? What saints are associated with a spear, or lance? . . . Wait a minute. Holy smokes, it can't be. There's just no way," I thought. Sure enough, right there in one of the four niches under the main dome of the basilica (most honored of places!) towers the soldier who pierced the heart of Jesus on the cross.[4]

I have since come to learn that the history of Longinus started with the apocryphal gospel of Nicodemus,[5] where this soldier referenced in John's gospel was named for the first time. The legend of Longinus indicates that his experience at the foot of the cross changed his life, prompting him to become not only a disciple of Jesus Christ, but more famously a teacher of the early church, and eventually leading him to a martyr's death. Apparently he experienced a total conversion of heart after realizing he had been sorely mistaken about this criminal, "Jesus of Nazareth, King of the Jews."

Let's think about this person in historical context. Longinus was a Roman soldier stationed to stand guard at an execution site to ensure that the criminals did indeed die as intended. Given his placement in Jerusalem, Longinus was likely an auxiliary soldier rather than a member of the legionaries, the more prestigious soldier class. Auxiliaries were not given the privilege of Roman citizenship because they were usually recruited from the hinterlands to do the less savory jobs within the Roman Empire. So let's imagine that Longinus was far

---

[4] Ironically, as this book goes to publication, the 2023 Indiana Jones movie *Dial of Destiny* has just been released, the plot of which opens with an attempt to retrieve the "Lance of Longinus," the sword used to pierce the side of Jesus as he hung dead on the cross in this passage of John. I am grateful to Lucasfilm for popularizing an otherwise exceptionally obscure religious figure!

[5] These writings by early Christians provide accounts of Jesus and the early church but are not included in the canonical texts of the New Testament used by the Roman Catholic, Eastern Orthodox, or Protestant churches since the fifth century. For an extensive discussion, I recommend Bart D. Ehrman and Zlatko Pleše's *The Apocryphal Gospels* (New York: Oxford University Press, 2011).

from home, working at a job that was badly paid, poorly esteemed, and oftentimes dangerous, with little to no knowledge of the crucified men that were his charge for the day.

If we backtrack a little in the Gospel of John and use only the account provided in chapter 19, we learn that the soldiers who crucified Jesus were pretty active in the three hours he hung on the cross. They stripped him of his clothes and cast lots to see who could keep them (v. 23-24), they witnessed the conversation between Jesus, his mother, and the disciple John (v. 26-27), they soaked a sponge with sour wine and fashioned a makeshift rod to raise it to his lips (v. 29-30), they heard Jesus' words in prayer (v. 30), they received Pontius Pilate's order to remove the bodies before sundown (v. 31), and they broke the legs of the other two criminals on the hill (v. 32). Finally, upon seeing Jesus already dead, Longinus decided that, rather than breaking his legs, he would stab him through the heart to make sure he was fully expired. This does not make it sound as if the soldier Longinus thought he was doing anything wrong. He was simply fulfilling his duty: executing criminals, doling out justice according to Roman law. In fact, he may have thought this gesture from the governor Pontius Pilate to be quite generous, this consent to remove the bodies before sundown in acquiescence to the religious customs of the Jews.

He was wrong about Jesus, though, and he came to learn that with one thrust of his spear.

For as long as I can remember, I have had a devotion to the Sacred Heart of Jesus. What that means is that I find spiritual strength and meaning, as well as personal applicability, in praying about (or more accurately, praying *with*) the love of God that is expressed through the heart of Jesus Christ. The "heart" is used in Western culture to represent love, value, intention, and sometimes even commitment. Consider phrases like these: "his heart just isn't in it," "she's all heart," "they really have a heart for the downtrodden," "he wears his heart on his sleeve," "the heart of the matter," and so on. When we speak about the heart, we are implying something central to a person, something essential to their character. So when we consider the heart of Jesus, or the Sacred Heart, Christian belief proposes that it represents everything there is to know about the love of God. What fills the heart of Jesus is demonstrated by his words, his actions, and his teachings, but in this gospel passage, we read of an experience with the physical anatomical heart of Jesus, and it is as spiritually beautiful as it is theologically valuable.

Jesus was already dead as verse 30 makes crystal clear. Humanity had already done every despicable thing possible to him—we had rejected him, plotted and schemed against him, lied about him, denied that we knew him, sold him out for money, abandoned him, beaten him, mocked him, tortured him, and finally killed him in the most humiliating and excruciating way possible. And then, once he was dead, we thrust a lance straight through his heart—*just to be sure*. Not a very flattering picture of the human response to the love of God given us in Christ Jesus.[6] And certainly not the picture-perfect ending to the story of the Incarnation of the Son of God one might expect. It's actually a pretty damning set of human behaviors, if you ask me. God the Father sent the Son to demonstrate once and for all who God is—a God of tenderness and mercy, unity and community—in a way that we could understand, in human countenance. *Surely,* the Trinity must have conspired, *they will come to understand and believe now. Surely they will accept my love this time, in this way, God-made-flesh.*

Uh, not so much.

---

[6] Lest the reader protest and say, "I never did that—'other people' like Peter and Judas and the Sanhedrin and the Romans did that!" I point you to a thirteenth-century admonition from St. Francis of Assisi's *Writings* (Philadelphia: Dolphin Press, 1906): "And even the demons did not crucify Him, but we together with them crucified Him and still crucify Him by taking delight in vices and sins" (*Admonitio*, 3.5, available at https://sacred-texts.com/chr/wosf/wosf03.htm). Also consider that the Christian services on Good Friday purposefully recommend that the congregation be the ones to shout, "Crucify him!" during the reading of the Passion.

God would have been perfectly justified in giving up on humanity right then and there, literally raining down hellfire on the whole ungrateful lot of us. What did God do instead? God stayed true to the Heart. When we rejected, denied, betrayed, and committed every other sort of sin, Jesus forgave us. When we killed him, he implored the Father's mercy. And when we thrust that lance through his heart, *just to be sure*, well, he did something unthinkable: he gave even more.

"Immediately blood and water flowed out" (v. 34).

This outpouring of blood and water has historically been interpreted as symbolic of two essential Christian theological realities:[7]

1. **The birth of the church:** "The origin and growth of the Church are symbolized by the blood and water which flowed from the open side of the crucified Jesus. For it was from the side of Christ as he slept the sleep of death upon the cross that there came forth the 'wondrous sacrament of the whole Church.' As Eve was formed from the sleeping Adam's side, so the Church was born from the pierced heart of Christ hanging dead on the cross."[8]

2. **The sacraments of baptism and Eucharist:** "The blood and water that flowed from the pierced side of the crucified Jesus are types of Baptism and the Eucharist, the sacraments of new life. From then on, it is possible 'to be born of water and the Spirit' in order to enter the Kingdom of God."[9]

---

[7] It is impossible to do justice to the breadth and depth of theological scholarship regarding this single Scripture verse. For those who are interested in a concise but thorough overview, I recommend Sebastian Carnazzo's doctoral dissertation, *Seeing Blood and Water: A Narrative-critical Study of John 19:34* (Washington, DC: Catholic University, 2011), available at https://cuislandora.wrlc.org/islandora/object/etd%3A143/datastream/PDF/view.

[8] *Catechism of the Catholic Church*, article 766.

[9] *Catechism of the Catholic Church*, article 1225.

We need not venture too far into the deep waters of ecclesiology or sacramentology to get a sense of the significance and import of this event. Jesus was dead—yet even in death, he continued to give, to create. His heart burst open, pouring out "living streams" of blood and water, flooding us with both new life (water) and the promise of unconditional love (blood). The water cleansed us of everything that came before, and the blood promised that Love conquers all—even death.

Hold on. Did you notice? The Heart of Jesus gave rebirth *even before Christ's resurrection!* And, as if that weren't enough, it is astonishing to note who the first recipient of this gift was. The first one to be washed clean and lovingly redeemed was the very perpetrator of the act, the sinner himself: the soldier Longinus.

Pause. And read that again: *the first one to be forgiven is the very one who is lashing out.*

Many times, this seems too much for me to bear. Can violence really be this easily forgiven, evil so quickly dismissed? What about admission of wrongdoing? What about retribution? What about taking the side of the victim?

This is a struggle with which I (and I am guessing many folks) have wrestled mightily on more than a few occasions. When I sit with this as a Christian, part of me questions God: *Really, God? In the very act of aggression, I'm supposed to pour out love? To the very person hurting me, you're asking me to shower forgiveness? What about an apology? What about battling evil? What about justice, for crying out loud?*[10]

To each of these questions raised in prayer, I have only ever intuited one answer from the Christian God: *I see your hurting, I feel your outrage. I hear your pain. Virginia, look at me. Look to my Heart and see. Learn from what you observe. Learn from*

---

[10] I address this painful and difficult experience more fully in chapter 7 of my book *Gifts from Friends We've Yet to Meet: A Memoir of Biblical Encounters* (Collegeville, MN: Liturgical Press, 2021).

what you receive. When I look, what I see is the heart of God, broken wide open. What I learn is that God is not unfamiliar with suffering, violence, and injustice. When we, therefore, experience them in our own lives, our compassionate God does, too. And the heart of Jesus, the Sacred Heart, responds to those experiences the same way, *every time*: with an outpouring of love. God cannot respond any other way—for God *is* love (1 John 4:8). This is the God I believe in as a Christian, but this is not a God to be admired; this is a God to be imitated.

Many people throughout history, both Christian and non-Christian alike, have not only understood this, but have lived and died because of this belief. In recent history, Mahatma Gandhi's commitment to nonviolence stands out as a shining example. When asked how he could continue to allow people to suffer as a result of following his teachings, he purportedly said, "Through our pain, we will make them see their injustice, and it will hurt [us] as all fighting hurts. But we cannot lose; we cannot."[11] He believed that violence and injustice are antithetical to being fully human; therefore, the only potential for converting violent and unjust systems lies in exposing them for the horror that they are, not meeting them in kind.

Just a few decades later, Dr. Martin Luther King Jr., inspired by Gandhi and deeply committed to following the example of Jesus Christ, eloquently described what this requires. In March 1961, he delivered a speech on what is meant by "loving our enemies":

> Love is the key to the solution of the problems of our world, love even for enemies. . . . The first thing that the individual must do in order to love his enemy is to develop the capacity to forgive with a naturalness and ease. If one does not have the capacity to forgive, he doesn't have the capacity to love. . . .
>
> I think this is what Jesus means when he says, "Love your enemies." Love is understanding, redemptive, creative good-

---

[11] Richard Attenborough (director), *Gandhi*, Columbia Pictures, 1982, film.

will for all. . . . [T]o return evil for evil only intensifies the existence of hate and evil in the universe. . . . Love serves to build up. Hate seeks destructive ends. Love seeks constructive ends. Hate seeks to annihilate. Love seeks to convert. Hate seeks to live in monologue. Love seeks to live in dialogue. . . . [T]here is something about love that can transform, that can change, that can arouse the conscience of the enemy.

We will match your capacity to inflict suffering by our capacity to endure suffering. We will meet your physical force with soul force. Do to us what you will, and we will still love you. . . . And one day we will win our freedom, but not only will we win freedom for ourselves, we will so appeal to your heart and conscience that we will win you in the process.[12]

One day, we will win you in the process.

This—*this*—is the message of the Heart of Jesus as it pours out blood and water upon the soldier Longinus. *You strike me through the heart, I flood you with water: be washed or be drowned—it is your choice. You pierce me through the heart, I pour out on you love: be redeemed or have blood on your hands—it is your choice. My gift is and will always be life and transformative love. Choose it. Receive it. Believe it.*[13]

Choose life, God tells us. "I have set before you life and death, the blessing and the curse. Choose life, then, that you and your descendants may live" (Deut 30:19). It's as if God is saying, "OK, friend, you're right. I've given you free will, you

---

[12] Martin Luther King Jr., *Loving Your Enemies*, audio transcription, sermon (Detroit, 1961), available at https://kinginstitute.stanford.edu/king-papers/documents/loving-your-enemies-sermon-delivered-detroit-council-churches-noon-lenten.

[13] Perhaps my all-time favorite artistic explication of this choice is through the characters Valjean and Javert from *Les Misérables*. Both are recipients of unconditional love. Valjean chooses to accept it and thus assents to the hard work of personal transformation; Javert cannot bear to accept the gift nor the conversion of heart required because it means he must admit that he was wrong and change his life accordingly.

can choose whatever you'd like. I'm giving you options—life or death, blessing or curse. Take your pick. You have the freedom to choose revenge, bitterness, resentment, retribution, punishment—or any cousin in that nasty family of death. But you also have the freedom to choose forgiveness, healing, hope, grace, mercy—and every cousin in my family of life. Make your choice. I won't force you, but I'll give you a big hint: *choose life*. It's a much better choice for you and for everyone else you love."

Choosing life, love, and forgiveness isn't condoning badness. It's not giving a stamp of approval to violence and evil. It is an act of faith and hope, acknowledging that the only way to conquer violence once and for all is through overflowing peace; that only goodness can ultimately defeat evil; and that in the end, love wins. And it wins *every time*.

This was likely not Longinus's belief when he showed up for duty at the foot of the cross that original Good Friday. The crucified Jesus did not look like he was winning. But then, the soldier's lance opened up the side of Christ and revealed how the Heart of Jesus will always respond to the worst of all human choices. Onto our worst mistakes, God pours out streams of life-giving water and floods of transforming love. Longinus was blessed to be the first to receive, the quickest to believe, and the most blessed one to admit, "O God, I was wrong."

From Longinus:

That day changed my life, changed the way I see, the way I think, what I believe. Heck, it changed everything. "Conversion" doesn't even come close to describing what happened in and through me. You see, I was a nobody, assigned to that hill because it was "dirty work," and I basically had no rank. I was just like the other guys—crass, selfish, snide. I couldn't tell you what we talked about as we waited for those three men to die, but I'll tell you this—it sure wasn't recognition of who Jesus of Nazareth was. Nope, we were completely oblivious. All I really cared about was getting the job done and getting out of there.

But then we got word that the Jews didn't want to have the bodies hanging past sundown, so we needed to accelerate the death process. Since Jesus was already gone, there was no need to expend the kind of energy it takes to break legs, so instead I thought I'd just quick-and-easy stab him to remove whatever last life-breath might still be in him.

I hadn't even removed the lance when I was flooded—and I literally mean flooded—by what came rushing out of his open side. I can't explain this, and I never would have believed it if I hadn't witnessed it myself, but two distinct streams flowed over me, starting at my arm and then covering my entire torso. Blood isn't supposed to flow out of a dead body, and I'd never seen a stream of water like that. But that's what it was—blood and water—flowing! Flowing out of his heart and into mine. And I know this will sound crazy to most people, but somehow he spoke. I didn't hear his voice, but he spoke to me—from beyond the bounds of death. And he told me, "Fear not, all things are now made new. You are made clean. You are beloved. It is finished."

It was more than a message; it was my name. That water and blood made me someone new, took everything that I had been before, and recreated me. I was a nobody when I started work that day, or so I thought. And I had thought this Jesus of Nazareth was just one more criminal sentenced to an awful death.

Boy, was I wrong.

Chapter 9: Cleopas[1]

Befriending Disappointment: The Gift of Presence

The road to Emmaus

---

[1] As mentioned in chapter 7, Christian traditions (including Orthodox) have long held that Cleopas and Clopas are likely one and the same person. Testaments from the early Christian chronicler Hegesippus the Nazarene (ca. 110–180 CE) and Eusebius of Caesarea (ca. 260–339 CE) propose that Clopas/Cleopas/Cleophas was brother to Joseph, making Cleopas an uncle to Jesus. Based on this, many Scripture scholars believe that the other Emmaus disciple could very well have been Cleopas's wife Mary, present at the foot of the cross in John 19:25. The conversation they engage with Jesus in this chapter's passage takes on a much more personal, familial tone when entertaining the possibility that the two Emmaus disciples may have been Jesus' aunt and uncle. For a fuller treatment of this background and history, I recommend Richard Bauckham, "The Relatives of Jesus," *Themelios* 21 (1996): 18–21, available at http://tgc-documents.s3.amazonaws.com/themelios/Themelios 21.2.pdf.

Two of [the disciples] were going to a village seven miles from Jerusalem called Emmaus, and they were conversing about all the things that had occurred. And it happened that while they were conversing and debating, Jesus himself drew near and walked with them, but their eyes were prevented from recognizing him. He asked them, "What are you discussing as you walk along?" They stopped, looking downcast. One of them, named Cleopas, said to him in reply, "Are you the only visitor to Jerusalem who does not know of the things that have taken place there in these days?" And he replied to them, "What sort of things?" They said to him, "The things that happened to Jesus the Nazarene, who was a prophet mighty in deed and word before God and all the people, how our chief priests and rulers both handed him over to a sentence of death and crucified him. But we were hoping that he would be the one to redeem Israel; and besides all this, it is now the third day since this took place. Some women from our group, however, have astounded us: they were at the tomb early in the morning and did not find his body; they came back and reported that they had indeed seen a vision of angels who announced that he was alive. Then some of those with us went to the tomb and found things just as the women had described, but him they did not see." And he said to them, "Oh, how foolish you are! How slow of heart to believe all that the prophets spoke! Was it not necessary that the Messiah should suffer these things and enter into his glory?" Then beginning with Moses and all the prophets, he interpreted to them what referred to him in all the scriptures.

As they approached the village to which they were going, he gave the impression that he was going on farther. But they urged him, "Stay with us, for it is nearly evening and the day is almost over." So he went in to stay with them. And it happened that, while he was with them at table, he took bread, said the blessing, broke it, and gave it to them. With that their eyes were opened and they recognized him, but he vanished from their sight. Then they said to each other, "Were not our hearts burning [within us] while he spoke to us on the way and opened the scriptures to us?" So they set out at once and returned to Jerusalem.

—*Luke 24:13-33*

The phrase, "but we had been hoping" in verse 21 gets me every time. Disappointment just stinks. I know, I know, there's no getting around it, "into each life some rain must fall," and all that, but still.[2] The crestfallen feeling that combines "ohhhhh," and "what the heck just happened?" quickly yields to a sense of "now what?" but not before forcing us to ask ourselves, "were we totally wrong the whole time?" It seems the two disciples on the road to Emmaus may have been wrestling with this exact question. When the stranger joins them in the midst of their conversation, they are able to give voice to their disappointment and confusion, and the one phrase that captures its entire essence: "but we had been hoping . . ."

We could intercept this feeling by jumping to the end of the story with a reassuring, "Yes, but look how it all turned out! Why dwell on the negative when we know the ending will be redemptive?" In reality, though, Cleopas and his companion did not have the least inkling that the end of their experience would be redemptive, so let's stay with them for a little while in their heart-brokenness and disappointment.

Hope is borne as a result of pain redeemed, but the inescapable prerequisite is that prior to the redemption of such experiences, they are experienced as painful! Pain, disappointment, and heartbreak may not be the most comfortable or

---

[2] Henry Wadsworth Longfellow, *Ballads and Other Poems* (Cambridge: 1842), 111–12.

pleasant of human emotions, but that does not disqualify them from being valuable gift-bearers for our souls.

My earliest memory of being disappointed by an important figure in my life goes all the way back to Christmas of 1979. I was eight years old and the only thing I wanted for Christmas was a lunchbox. All my friends had shiny, beautiful lunchboxes with a matching thermos inside and a snazzy flip-lock on the front. I, on the other hand, carried my lunch each day in a brown paper bag. I was required to keep the bag for a week's worth of use, so every day after lunch, I would fold it up when I finished eating and tuck it into my jumper belt. (This provided quite a challenge, I might add, when playing keep-away at recess, as I had to run while grasping my belly to ensure I didn't lose the bag!) I thought my odds of getting aforementioned lunchbox were pretty good since it was literally the only thing I asked for that year. Our family Christmas list consisted of a huge piece of butcher paper taped to the refrigerator, marked off with squares for each of the children living at home. In my 3x4 inch section, I wrote in large print, "Lunchbox (any kind but HOLLY HOBBIE)."[3] My eight-year-old self believed I was too grown up for such a childish design as Holly Hobbie, so I wanted to ensure that my parents respected my maturity by purchasing Snoopy, Scooby Doo, or Star Wars if I was lucky. It mattered little as long as it was not Holly Hobbie. Anything but that, please.

Apparently my dad (my poor dad) was responsible for shopping for me that year. Since he could not take the list with him to the stores, and since neither cell phones nor digital cameras existed yet, all he had with him on his shopping excursion was his memory and a furiously scribbled note to himself: "lunch box for Virginia—Holly Hobbie." He went to

---

[3] For those on whom the cultural reference is lost, Holly Hobbie was a fictional character popular with many children in the 1970s. The design consisted basically of the profile of a cat-loving, rag dress-wearing little girl in a giant bonnet.

four different stores to make sure he could find me a Holly Hobbie lunchbox. (You can imagine how this story ends.)

Come Christmas Eve, I was so excited I could hardly sit still. A day earlier, I had surreptitiously spied my present under the tree, shaking it to ensure that it was, indeed, the booty I hoped for. Two full days of eager anticipation, wondering if it might be Wonder Woman? Maybe it'll be—oh, dare I hope?—the Muppets! So finally the time arrived for gift opening, and I ripped the paper off as fast as I could, only to discover . . . the dreaded blue-bonneted girl.

As I have thought about this moment over the years, I have shifted from remembering the intensity of that anticipation and let-down to imagining the experience from my dad's perspective. I actually doubt that he had his full attention on me simply because there was so much ripping and shouting and jumping and throwing going on in the room. I can't really imagine that he was zeroed in on me and my reaction. At least I hope not. Because what he would have seen would have broken his heart, I'm sure. Me, originally so excited and grateful and eager—and then, so quickly distressed upon opening the gift that represented his time, attention, effort and, put simply, *love*. I don't think I wailed, but I am certain I at least moped. My father's efforts had missed the mark I had set, leaving my eight-year-old self badly disappointed, but only because that young girl couldn't see past her own perspective to recognize the presence of deep, abiding love in her very midst, a love with no motivation except itself. A love that wanted desperately to please a daughter—and who seemed to have failed in the attempt. Or did he? That Holly Hobbie lunchbox is the only Christmas gift of my childhood that I can still remember . . . and my father's dedication to procuring it has now made literary record. Way to go, Dad!

People disappoint us all the time: important people, powerful people, people who should know better, people who should do better, people we look up to, people who look up to us, our friends, our parents, our children, our grandchildren, our public servants—even our God. Yes, what Cleopas and the other disciple were saying on the road to Emmaus was that Jesus had disappointed them. Their hopes had been dashed.

They weren't the first ones, you know. Jesus disappointed John the Baptist as we saw in chapter 5, he disappointed the rich young man, the people of his hometown in Nazareth, and especially (and consistently) the religious leaders of his time. (See Matt 11:2-3; 19:22; 13:54-57; 15:1-2, respectively.) It is no heresy to admit being disappointed by God—nor does it imply faithlessness.

I am humbled to say that many of the students I have taught through the years have stayed in touch. As they continued their life journeys through college, then marriage, family-building, and career, some have shared with me the heartbreak of their lives. Infertility, cancer, debilitating accident, natural disaster, wrongful arrest—these are just a sampling of the difficulties they have experienced. "Disappointing" seems way too tame a word to characterize our emotional response in the face of these realities. And yet, when I ask them if they've considered whether they are upset with God, almost universally they recoil at such a thought. "I didn't know it was OK to admit that," one said. "Isn't that kind of sacrilegious?" from another. "I'm not really mad at God," insisted a third, but then more tearfully, "I just don't understand why he would let this happen."

God can take our honesty. As a matter of fact, I am a firm believer that God desires to hear us voice it, not for God's own sake but for ours. Just as Jesus asked Cleopas and his companion on the road to Emmaus to tell him about their disappointment, he asks us, too: "What sorts of things are you so upset about?" And then, he listens to our heartbroken response as he walks right beside us. Unless and until we can be truthful about what "we had been hoping," we may never have the opportunity to recognize God in our midst, on the journey with us every step of the way. But once we do share the full story with him (again, not because it is news to him but because there is something crucial for ourselves in narrating the reality), then we have the chance to put our story in the context of something bigger, grander, fuller, and more beautiful. Then—and I would argue *only* then—can the bitterness of our disappointment be transformed into something hopeful and restorative.

When my niece Katie was about four years old, my brother Matt took her for the prescribed inoculations at the pediatrician's office. She was the most easy-going kid you can imagine, nonplussed about having to eat vegetables, stoic in the face of scraped knees and elbows, comfortable with chaos. She sat in the doctor's office with her dad, nodding agreement when he said, "OK, Katie, the nurses are going to give you three shots. It's going to hurt a little bit, but it will be over fast."

"OK, Dad," she said, completely at ease, knowing that her dad was right there so she was sure to be safe and protected. In point of fact, she had no idea what was coming. My brother, on the other hand, was a wreck. Two nurses came in with three syringes. They asked Katie to sit in the chair between their stools. She hopped up obediently as they prepared to stick both arms simultaneously with the first two shots. Matt was asked if he wanted to wait in the lobby.

"No, I'll stay here and try to distract her," said my brother, ever the optimist. "Knock-knock."

"Who's there?" chimed Katie on cue.

Then the two shots went in. She was originally just startled and confused, forgetting the joke and trying to jump out of the chair to get to her dad. Then, Katie-who-never-cried registered the pain and started to scream, realizing that there were enemies on the attack and she needed to escape. She looked directly at her father, trying unsuccessfully to convince him to eliminate the aggressors, to keep her safe from what she was experiencing as terrible harm. All she got in return was a father who was sitting idly by, *letting this happen to her*. (Believe me, my brother was much more distraught that day than his daughter.) Then, one of the nurses brought the third syringe close while the other tried to calm Katie. If my niece's first look at her dad had registered confusion morphing into pleading, her last look became one of absolute betrayal. She no longer saw her father as the one who would protect her, but as the one who was refusing to do anything to stop the pain. When the shots had all been administered, Katie did not want to be picked up by my brother. She stopped screaming, but the tears still flowed as she sat there in the chair too big for her small body. She may not have wanted to go home in the company of her dad, but she had no place else to go, and no one else to go to. He was her only option. The problem was that in her tiny person mind, from the perspective of her immediate experience, he had become untrustworthy.

Now you, dear reader, have the advantage of understanding exactly what was happening in this scenario—as did the nurses, as did my brother. But the understanding that results from *our* experience and perspective did nothing then—and would still do nothing now—to help, comfort, or soothe the mind and heart of a child in the midst of such an experience. My now-thirty-two-year-old niece Katie doesn't even have a memory of this event, but my brother's recollection is crystal clear.

Would he do it all over again, just the same? When I asked him this question recently, I suggested that in a "redo" he could leave her with the nurses and remove himself completely from the situation in order to come rushing to the rescue as the hero in the end. Matt pondered this for a moment before he said that he would never do that. No, if he had to do it again, he would do the same thing—and for one simple reason. He would still want to be the one who stayed with her through it. He would not be willing to leave her alone or to let her imagine he had abandoned her during such a time.

This, my friends, is how our God walks with us on our journey. Please do not misunderstand me: I am in no way implying that every painful thing that happens to us is for our own good (like inoculations are for children). What I am stating as my firm belief is that when we are stricken with the pain or heartache that comes with the tough parts of life, our God is not standing idly by, powerless to do anything about it or worse yet, unwilling. Nor is God saying, "OK, you get through this and I'll see you on the other side." No, our God is right there with us, refusing to leave us alone in our pain, staying with us all the way through as we wriggle and question, wail and accuse. If it seems God is absent or deaf or unfeeling in response, we might look to the example of Cleopas, and just come out and say it plainly. We might dare to speak our disappointment, express our confusion and sense of betrayal, honestly tell God what it feels like. Wouldn't we be just as surprised as those two disciples on the Emmaus road if, in response, God provided for us an experience of blessing and recognition?

Before believers in Jesus were called Christians, they were known as "followers of the Way," presumably because Jesus had said, "I am the way and the truth, and the life" (John 14:6). The story of the disciples' encounter with the risen Jesus on the road to Emmaus reminds us that when we are "on our way" in life, we are joined each and every day by him who *is* the Way. May the security of Jesus' presence and promise set our hearts on fire, even—or especially—when we have difficulty recognizing his presence in our very midst.

From Cleopas:

I'm not gonna lie. I was ticked. And hurt. And scared. But mostly I remember feeling let down. I had put all my proverbial eggs in the "Jesus basket," so when things happened in Jerusalem the way they did and he died so brutally and, well, so *willingly*, I didn't know what to think. I didn't know what to do. And I certainly didn't know what to believe. That's what we were talking about on our way to Emmaus—how to go on. Think about it: what were we supposed to believe in when everything we believed in had died?

Then, this stranger showed up and asked us what we were talking about. It was hard to imagine how anyone could have not known what had occurred. But that's how grief is, I guess. My whole world had been shattered, but the rest of the world went on as usual.

To be honest, it felt good to talk about it, to relive everything as we walked, to remember everything Jesus had done, everything he had promised . . . to remember *him*.

Then, this stranger just started preaching the Scripture, connecting everything we had said about our experience—*every single thing*—to the Torah, the prophets, the psalms, pretty much all of salvation history. It was absolutely amazing. And it sparked something new. No, that's not right. It fanned into flame the hope that we thought was dead. So he came in and stayed with us, and it was when we were sharing dinner that everything clicked. He repeated the exact same ritual and blessing of the bread as he had the night he was arrested. Just like that, we both knew. And as soon as I recognized him, he was gone. He disappeared with what I swear was a little grin, almost like, "Do you get it now?" We looked at each other and said, "We've got to go back!" and we took off running.

You know what's funny? All these years since then, the meaning of that encounter just keeps getting richer and richer. He was with us the whole time. Listening to us, walking with us. Even if he hadn't stayed, even if we hadn't recognized him, it wouldn't have changed that fact. He was with us and we didn't recognize him for a really long time. You know what that tells me? That his presence isn't dependent on my sense of it. I don't always *feel* God's closeness, for sure. But every once in a while, if I stop to pay attention, I'll sense something more than myself within me, something deep and rich and trustworthy. I can't necessarily explain it and I sure can't prove it, but it is real and true, and I know—*ah, he's here.*

Chapter 10: Peter

Befriending Failure: The Gift of Authority

The repentance of St. Peter

[After the resurrection,] Simon Peter said, "I am going fishing." [The other disciples] said to him, "We also will come with you." So they went out and got into the boat, but that night they caught nothing. When it was already dawn, Jesus was standing on the shore; but the disciples did not realize that it was Jesus. Jesus said to them, "Children, have you caught anything to eat?" They answered him, "No." So he said to them, "Cast the net over the right side of the boat and you will find something." So they cast it, and were not able to pull it in because of the number of fish. So the disciple whom Jesus loved said to Peter, "It is the Lord." When Simon Peter heard that it was the Lord, he tucked in his garment, for he was lightly clad, and jumped into the sea. The other disciples came in the boat, for they were not far from shore, only about a hundred yards, dragging the net with the fish. When they climbed out on shore, they saw a charcoal fire with fish on it and bread. Jesus said to them, "Bring some of the fish you just caught." So Simon Peter went over and dragged the net ashore full of one hundred fifty-three large fish. Even though there were so many, the net was not torn. Jesus said to them, "Come, have breakfast." And none of the disciples dared to ask him, "Who are you?" because they realized it was the Lord. Jesus came over and took the bread and gave it to them, and in like manner the fish. This was now the third time Jesus was revealed to his disciples after being raised from the dead.

When they had finished breakfast, Jesus said to Simon Peter, "Simon, son of John, do you love me more than these?" He said to him, "Yes, Lord, you know that I love you." He said to him, "Feed my lambs." He then said to him a second time, "Simon, son of John, do you love me?" He said to him, "Yes, Lord, you know that I love you." He said to him, "Tend my sheep." He said to him the third time, "Simon, son of John, do you love me?" Peter was distressed that he had said to him a third time, "Do you love me?" and he said to him, "Lord, you know everything; you know that I love you." [Jesus] said to him, "Feed my sheep.

> Amen, amen, I say to you, when you were younger, you used to dress yourself and go where you wanted; but when you grow old, you will stretch out your hands, and someone else will dress you and lead you where you do not want to go." He said this signifying by what kind of death he would glorify God. And when he had said this, he said to him, "Follow me."
>
> Peter turned and saw the disciple following whom Jesus loved. . . . When Peter saw him, he said to Jesus, "Lord, what about him?" Jesus said to him, "What if I want him to remain until I come? What concern is it of yours? You follow me."
>
> —*John 21:3-22*

Simon Peter's life certainly provides plenty of content to discuss failure. Peter was not exactly the brightest crayon in the box according to Scripture. He protested when Jesus told him to "put into deep water and lower the nets for a catch" (Luke 5:4), he blundered his response to Jesus' transfiguration by saying, "let's build a tent here!" (see Matt 17:4), he consistently misunderstood or misinterpreted Jesus' teachings (see Matt 15:15, 18:21), he sank in the sea due to his lack of faith (Matt 14:30), he resisted Jesus' lessons (John 13:8), he fell asleep in the Garden of Gethsemane (Matt 26:40), he resorted to violence in the last hours of Jesus' life (John 18:10), and he denied knowing Jesus after swearing he would die rather than do so (Matt 26:35).

Wow, not a great résumé for the first pope! And those are just a few of the unflattering examples running all through the four gospels of Peter's failures, without even touching the Acts of the Apostles! So why in the world did Jesus choose to single out Peter for leadership, even going so far as to entrust the authority of the entire Christian project to him? The classic Scripture passage of Peter's appointment comes from Matthew. In chapter 16, when Jesus asked the disciples, "Who do you say that I am?" Peter's answer was a beautiful testament of faith: "You are the Messiah, the Son of the living God." In response to Peter's A+ answer, Jesus promised him, "I will give you the keys to the kingdom of heaven" and it is upon this rock of you, Peter, that I will build my church.[1] I often wonder if the other disciples thought at the time (as I still do today at times), "This guy? You're basing everything on *this* guy?"

Sure enough, in his very next breath, Peter "took Jesus aside and began to rebuke him" for the predictions he was making of his own suffering and death. Yup, there he is, that's our boy, taking an absolutely beautiful moment and turning it into a fiasco. Can you *imagine* having the nerve to rebuke the Son of God?! What in the world was Peter thinking? Did he imagine that the authority of the kingdom was effective immediately and it extended to challenging the Second Person of the Trinity? Jesus took no time to set the story straight, answering Peter with the scathing response of: "Get behind me, Satan! You are an obstacle to me!" (Matt 16:15-23).

This is Peter. *This guy.* The guy with the keys in his hand and his foot in his mouth. The guy Jesus named his successor in one breath and Satan in the next. The guy who knows what it is to believe. And to fail. The guy who demonstrated for all of us the fact that failure—even *big-time* failure—shouldn't surprise us because it sure doesn't surprise God.

My high school religion teacher was a burly, rosy-cheeked nun from the Bronx, Sister Christine. She wore a full-length

---

[1] Peter is actually a nickname given to Simon by Jesus. In this passage as well as in John 1:42, Jesus names Simon "Cephas," the Aramaic word for "rock," translated into "Petros" in Greek and "Peter" in English. It might seem odd to our contemporary sensibilities, but the original texts are clear: when Jesus entrusted his authority to a human successor, he did so with a nickname equivalent to what we might use today as "Rocky."

habit which only barely disguised her linebacker frame, and she had a booming voice that rang out equally often with uproarious laughter and detention distribution. She was teaching Catholic sacraments one day, talking about confession and the need for a good examination of conscience in order to truly get a handle on where we needed forgiveness. It pushed every guilt button we fourteen-year-old girls had, and we proceeded to badger her with dozens of nervous questions about whether or not our souls were in mortal peril.

"What if, after I leave the confession box, I remember that I forgot to say something? Should I go back?"

"If I didn't know it was a sin when I did it but now I do, does it count?"

"Should I confess something if I got away with it?"

"Is there anything that can't be forgiven?"

"Will the priest think I'm a bad person?"

Finally, after patiently responding to our concerns for at least half the class, she stood up, crossed her arms across her body, and said, "Listen, ladies. I know you're scared. I know you think you've really messed some stuff up. But here's the deal. I've lived a lot longer than you, I've had a lot more time to mess stuff up. I wasn't born a nun, you know. I grew up in the rough-and-tumble world of 'da Bronx.' I was a teenager just like you, and the stuff you dolls are worried about is nothing compared to my own history. So here's what I want to tell you. If you are worried that something you've done is unforgiveable, that you are just the worst of the worst and you imagine God will be repulsed at the sight of you, then think about this. Imagine yourself at the end of your life reaching the gates of heaven and encountering St. Peter face-to-face. Imagine that he greets you with a big clipboard and says, 'Why, hello there. Welcome to eternity, pleasure to have you. Let's just take a look here and find out where you belong. Oh, I see. Well, it seems you did pretty well most of your life, but wow, that summer of 1985, that was a doozy. It left a pretty substantial mark.

Heaven is filled with saints, you know. So, do you have anything to say about those marks and failures?' Ladies, if that's what Peter says to you as he stands before you swinging the keys to the gate of heaven, this is what you do. You look him straight in the eye, stand up straight and tall, and say, 'Just one thing: cock-a-doodle-do!' I guarantee he will let you right in."

Yes, Peter made plenty of mistakes, no question about it. But you know what else? He never let any of those mistakes stop him. Peter is the epitome of the Japanese proverb, "Fall down seven times, stand up eight."[2] When he rebuked Jesus and was told, "Get behind me, Satan!" what did Peter do? He stopped talking and fell in line behind Jesus. When Jesus saved Peter from the roaring waves because his lack of faith had caused him to sink, we must remember that Peter had been the only apostle to *get out of the boat* and walk on water! (Matt 14:28-31). And when, in chapter 18 of John's gospel, Peter so fearfully denied even knowing Jesus in the courtyard of the high priest, we must follow the trajectory of the story all the way to its completion in chapter 21, as excerpted above.

The context of this "breakfast on the beach" passage cannot be overlooked. This event took place after the resurrection of Jesus, when the apostles were trying to make sense of all that had happened. Peter, the leader of the apostle pack, made the uninspiring decision to return to a pastime he knew: fishing. The scene that unfolded was reminiscent of Peter's initial call in Luke 5, when Jesus told Peter to lower his nets after a night of unsuccessful fishing. When Peter did so, the number of fish he caught was overwhelming. So in this scene, when an apparent stranger called from the shore with an instruction to lower the nets, resulting in another overwhelming catch, Peter recognized what was happening. Leaving fish, boats, and companions behind, he could not wait to get to shore to be with Jesus.

---

[2] "七転び八起き" transliterates, "Nana korobi ya oki."

Wait a minute. Really? Peter, the same guy who only days earlier had denied Jesus and bolted, hiding from the Roman and Jewish authorities so as not to suffer the same fate, went running *toward* Jesus?

Exactly. This is the Peter I know and love. This is the one who got it wrong just as often as he got it right, who had the worst case of foot-in-mouth disease ever known to humankind, whose credentials left much to be desired—and who was designated by Jesus himself to be the leader of the church. I used to think that Jesus made this choice in spite of Peter's failures and weakness. I have come to believe that Jesus made this choice *because of* Peter's failures and weakness.[3]

Peter is the one who is stationed at the Pearly Gates; Peter is the one with the "keys to heaven." Imagine if we were greeted instead by Mary, Jesus' mother, who was sinless her whole life long. How different an encounter that would be; we certainly couldn't crow like a rooster to appeal to her sense of compassion! No, Jesus entrusted Peter with the role of heavenly gatekeeper, and Peter certainly understands what it is to have lived an imperfect life, to have had an imperfect faith. The story of Peter's life has been immortalized for centuries, and at least half of those stories highlight his failures in all their embarrassing glory. What was it about Peter that allowed him to be so comfortable accepting his own flaws? I tend to think it was his utter love for God partnered with his belief that Jesus revealed exactly who God is: a God of unfailing mercy.

Mercy: this concept is difficult to understand, especially when our sins seem so big and bad and damning. An allegory might help.

I once showed up to God's office, wondering what mercy meant. God said, "Mercy means that I love you, that's all."

---

[3] One of my favorite pieces of artwork is *The Repentance of St. Peter*, by Gerard Seghers (ca. 1650), pictured at the start of this chapter. It depicts Peter as an old man, deep in contemplation with two items in the background: a ring of keys and a rooster, symbolizing both his authority and his failure.

"Well, I've known lots of types of love in life. What's your love like?" I asked.

"My love is unconditional," God replied.

"Oh. So you can forgive me because your love is so big," I concluded.

"Yes, but not in the way you're imagining it. You seem to be comparing the size of your sin to the size of my love."

"I don't understand."

"A comparison like that doesn't make sense simply because the immensity and scale of my love is incomprehensible," God said. "Let me try to help you. Imagine this. My love for you is represented by every created thing that has ever existed—flowers and ocean, earth and sky, every living thing and every person to ever breathe, sun and moon, stars and galaxies, the universe and everything in it."

"OK, that's *really* big. And I seem small in comparison. I get that."

"Right, but we're just getting started. Now consider one grain of sand as it exists right now on this one day on one beach in one city in one country on this one planet in this one solar system in this one galaxy. Got it?"

"Uh, kind of. One grain of sand."

"That one grain of sand is sin. And everything else is my merciful love. Does that make it easier to imagine that I forgive you?"

"That *one* grain of sand is all my sin? And you're looking at it from the perspective of all created things—ever?"

"Not quite. That one grain of sand isn't *your* sin. That one grain of sand is the collection of sins from every person throughout every time and place for all of human history—past, present, and future."

"Ah," said I, steeped more in mystery and awe than in understanding.

"That's a start," said God.

Our failures and sinfulness contained in a grain of sand and subsumed into the eternal ocean of God's mercy: that is what Peter believed. Peter's unshakeable confidence in Jesus' forgiveness extended even to his most awful mistakes—and to the most awful mistakes of *everyone else, too*. I wonder if that wasn't precisely the source of Jesus' confidence in giving Peter his authority.

Think for a moment about one of your greatest flops. Maybe it was a colossal mistake that had ripple effects beyond yourself (I am remembering a ninth-inning left-field fly ball that would have sealed a district championship for my team . . . if I had caught the darn thing). Or maybe it was not so dramatic but still had enough import to remain even now in your memory bank (like forgetting an anniversary). Whatever the goof, I propose something for your consideration: do you feel as if you gained a certain level of wisdom from the experience? Do you sense a kind of authority to speak to similar situations when they happen to other people? I don't mean a prideful air that gives license to lord your hard-won knowledge over someone else. I mean the type of authority that recognizes the look of dejection or humiliation in someone else's eyes and gently says, "Let me tell you a story."

One night I was barbecuing shish-kebabs on a brand-new grill. They were beautiful to behold—green peppers, pineapple chunks, cherry tomatoes, pearl onions, and jumbo shrimp. I had marinated them all day long, had preheated the grill to the perfect temperature, and had arranged them in flawless symmetry across each skewer. I was carefully placing them on the grill to ensure that the char marks would cross the food exactly as I wanted for aesthetic purposes, when I realized I forgot to turn on the rice cooker. I closed the lid and ran inside to tend to the rice, assuming all would be well. *Wrong.* The new grill captured heat much better than the old one had, and with a greased rack and a closed lid, the food must have caught fire. That was the only conclusion I could draw because I returned a few minutes later and opened the lid, finding that all that was left were the metal skewers. The fire was so hot that it consumed everything in its vicinity, leaving only a few green pepper bits dangling across the burners.

In that dreadful moment, I considered running away. I had been bragging all day long about those dumb kebabs and now the only the thing on the menu was humble pie. As I picked up the phone to call for pizza, someone pulled burgers out of the freezer and suggested we make use of that really hot fire to speed-cook a different entrée instead. I stepped aside to let her take the role of chief grill master, but she just handed me the plate of burgers. "You, my friend, know the power of that fire better than anyone else. Have at it!" She was right. From that point forward, I felt like quite the authority on the power of that grill, even if the wisdom was hard-won.

That's the whole point: failure has the power to make us wise if we let it. In the case of Peter, his blunders, big and small, readied him for the authority entrusted to him by Jesus Christ. Jesus didn't see Peter as perfect (he wasn't), he saw him as faithful. Jesus didn't expect that Peter would cease making mistakes (he didn't), he expected Peter would learn from the mistakes he made. Peter was a flawed believer, a flawed follower, and a flawed leader. In one sense, the only thing Peter got right every time was the way he failed. Each time he messed up, he returned to Christ—*immediately*. Fall seven times, get up eight. Peter knew Jesus, *really* knew him—and he trusted that Jesus knew him. That didn't remove Peter's blemishes or idiosyncratic screw-ups. It redeemed them.

Looking at the Scripture passage chosen for this chapter, there are so many aspects of the dialogue between Peter and Jesus that I love, but recently my favorite part has been the end.[4] Jesus and Peter had just finished a truly beautiful con-

---

[4] I provide a much fuller look at this exchange between Peter and Jesus, including linguistic context, scriptural theology, and personal application in my book *Forgiveness, Choosing to Receive and to Give* (Collegeville, MN: Liturgical Press, 2019).

versation, recognized by most Scripture scholars as being Jesus' three-fold expression of forgiveness for Peter's three-fold expression of denial. Jesus had reaffirmed Peter's authority over "the flock," reminding him that his authority was based on love and service. Finally, Jesus had concluded this powerful dialogue with the same words with which he first called Peter: *follow me*. It is a rich, tender, deeply personal exchange demonstrating Jesus' profound love and trust of Peter. How did Peter respond? The exact way we have come to expect he would. Verses 20-21 reveal the Peter we have known consistently throughout the entire gospel. He looked over his shoulder at someone else (presumably John) and wanted to know, "OK, great. But what about him, that fella over there who seems to be your favorite? What's he gonna get?"

Oh, Peter, how I love thee. Let me count the ways. Even after you were called by Jesus, even after you were singled out among the Twelve for leadership, even after you were given the authority not just of the church on earth but of heaven in eternity, even after you were forgiven for failing Jesus in his darkest hour, even after you were reminded of who you are and how deeply you are known and loved—even after *all that*, you still didn't completely get it.

And I am so grateful to you for not getting it!

Peter is me; Peter is you; Peter is all of us. Even after all the ways God gives to us, loves us, forgives us, we still don't always get it. We still want to know, "What about them? What about the other person over there, the other things I've done, the other options I might have, the other possibilities that might come down the line?"

And God says, forcefully: *you follow me*.

I imagine Jesus saying this to Peter with something of an eyeroll or heavy sigh, but nonetheless, God's response to all our failures and ongoing backtracking is always the same: "Just stop talking, stop looking at other people to see if they have it better, and *you* follow *me*, all right? Can we try that?"

"But . . ." I protest.
"Nope," God persists.
"What if . . ." I continue.
"Did you hear me?" God asks.
"Can I . . .?"
"Virginia."
"Wait, just . . ." I continue.
"Stop. Listen: *you follow me*," God emphatically says. "Take a page from Peter's playbook, would you please? Trust boldly, fail miserably, return faithfully, and *for heaven's sake*, just follow me."

From Peter:

Words are not my strong suit, so I'll keep this short. Look at him, that's all you have to do. He tried to tell me that all throughout my life. When I was fishing that very first day, when I was walking on the sea toward him (can you believe that, by the way?), when I was talking with the girl in the courtyard the night before he died, even that last encounter on the beach. He said it over and over: "Eyes on me. Keep your eyes on me." I always understood it and I always believed it. But it's awfully hard to do. So when I forgot or failed or even just didn't want to, he waited. And when I got over myself and returned to him, there he was—still waiting for me. That's the key, friends. It's not about our faithfulness, really; it's about his. Keep your eyes on that, keep your heart attached to that, and you've got the key to everything.

Afterword

Life is hard. None of us escapes it unscathed. We can make some royal messes and do some pretty significant damage along the way. Hopefully, if you've made it to the end of this book, you are able to acknowledge this element of our common humanity with a greater gentleness—or at least with deeper reflection. We have spent ten chapters considering our own foibles and faltering faith, accompanied by gospel characters who assure us, "Oh, honey. We've been there. Don't be so hard on yourself. You're just fine. Now come on, don't wallow and be all 'Woe is me, I'm such a terrible sinner.' Get up; you've got work to do."

The next step is harder, and where this book ends, the real spiritual work begins: giving to every other person in our lives the same mercy, gentleness, good humor, and acceptance God has given us. If God smiles upon us in our error and sin (and God does), so are we called to do the same for all those who "trespass against us." God is not "my" father or "your" father—God is *Our Father*. And that means that you and I are family. We belong to each other. Let us pray for the grace to live according to that truth—every single day.

Acknowledgments

Special thanks to all the teachers of my life who have made this type of book possible, especially:

Ruth—finally I have written about our friend Peter. Thank you for your persistent encouragement.

Jerry and Vern—you have accompanied me as spiritual directors through some of my most difficult years. Thank you for teaching me patience, trust, and faith.

Mary, Jane, and Kate—the craft of writing became a love of mine through each of you. Thank you for your skill, your critiques, and your passion.

My students and directees—teachers learn more from their students than they could ever impart. Thank you for leading me closer to truth, goodness, and beauty every single day.

And to Jesus Christ, the Master Teacher. I am still learning. Thank you for never failing me.

Illustrations

The Meeting of Zechariah and Elizabeth (1611–1654),
by Francesco Guarino. Sant' Agata Irpina, near Solofra, Gravina di Puglia. Sothebys, New York.

The Death of St. Joseph (ca. 1900), by Joseph Sibbel.
Saint Francis Xavier College Church, St. Louis, Missouri.

St. Andrew and St. Peter (1480–1488), by Fernando Gallego.
University of Arizona Museum of Art, Tucson.

Martha and Mary (ca. 1620), by Orazio Gentileschi. Alte Pinakothek, Munich. © José Luiz Bernardes Ribeiro / CC BY-SA 4.0.

John the Baptist in Prison, by Chrispijn van den Broeck (1501–1600). Royal Library of Belgium.

The Kiss of Judas (16th century). Lower Rhine, Germany. Gift of J. Pierpont Morgan, 1916.

Pietà (1499; Florence, Italy), by Michelangelo. St. Peter's Basilica, Vatican.

St. Longinus, by Gian Lorenzo Bernini (1598–1680). St. Peter's Basilica, Vatican.

The Road to Emmaus (17th century), by Claes Moeyaert. Metropolitan Museum of Art, New York.

The Repentance of St. Peter (1603–1651), by Gerard Seghers. Louvre Museum, Paris.

Bibliography

Attenborough, Richard (director). *Gandhi*. Columbia Pictures, Goldcrest Production, 1982, film.

Atwal, Sanj. "Prince Harry's Spare Becomes Fastest-Selling Non-Fiction Book Ever." *Guinness World Records* (January 13, 2023). Available at https://www.guinnessworldrecords.com/news/2023/1/prince-harrys-spare-becomes-fastest-selling-non-fiction-book-ever-732915.

Balthasar, Hans Urs von. *Dare We Hope "That All Men Be Saved"?* San Francisco: Ignatius Press, 1988.

Balthasar, Hans Urs von. *Heart of the World*. San Francisco: Ignatius Press, 1979.

Barber, Richard W. *The Holy Grail: Imagination and Belief*. Cambridge, MA: Oxford University Press, 2004.

Bauckham, Richard. "The Relatives of Jesus." *Themelios* 21 (1996): 18–21. Available at http://tgc-documents.s3.amazonaws.com/themelios/Themelios21.2.pdf.

Brown, Raymond. "The Passion According to John." *Worship* 49 (2013): 126–34.

Carnazzo, Sebastian. *Seeing Blood and Water: A Narrative-critical Study of John 19:34*. Washington, DC: Catholic University, 2011, doctoral dissertation. Available at https://cuislandora.wrlc.org/islandora/object/etd%3A143/datastream/PDF/view.

Catechism of the Catholic Church. 2nd ed. Washington, DC: United States Catholic Conference—Libreria Editrice Vaticana, 1997.

Coughlin, Sean. "The Enduring Anguish of Being the Royal 'Spare.'" *BBC News* online (January 7, 2023). Available at https://www.bbc.com/news/uk-64185317.

Ehrman, Bart D., and Zlatko Pleše. *The Apocryphal Gospels*. New York: Oxford University Press, 2011.

Elgvin, Torleif. "The Messiah Who Was Cursed on the Tree." *Themelios* 22 (1997): 14–21.

Francis of Assisi. *Writings*. Philadelphia: Dolphin Press, 1906. Available at https://sacred-texts.com/chr/wosf/wosf03.htm.

Herbers, Virginia. *Forgiveness, Choosing to Receive and to Give*. Collegeville, MN: Liturgical Press, 2019.

Herbers, Virginia. *Gifts from Friends We've Yet to Meet: A Memoir of Biblical Encounters*. Collegeville, MN: Liturgical Press, 2021.

Kent, William. "Judas Iscariot." *The Catholic Encyclopedia*, vol. 8. New York: Robert Appleton, 1910. Available at http://www.newadvent.org/cathen/08539a.htm.

Kierkegaard, Søren. *The Sickness Unto Death*. Princeton, NJ: Princeton University Press, 1980.

King, Jr., Martin Luther. *Loving Your Enemies*. Audio transcription, sermon. Detroit, 1961. Available at https://kinginstitute.stanford.edu/king-papers/documents/loving-your-enemies-sermon-delivered-detroit-council-churches-noon-lenten.

Lewis, C. S. *The Great Divorce*. New York: Harper One, 1946.

Longfellow, Henry Wadsworth. *Ballads and Other Poems*. Cambridge: 1842.

Meier, John P. "The Circle of the Twelve." *Journal of Biblical Literature* 116 (Winter 1997): 635–72.

Miller, Jerome. "Wound Made Fountain: Toward a Theology of Redemption." *Theological Studies* 70 (September 2009): 525–54.

Rahner, Karl. *Servants of the Lord*. New York: Herder and Herder, 1968.

Rolheiser, Ronald. *Sacred Fire*. New York: Image, 2014.

Saint Louis Counseling. "I've Been Wronged! Do I Have to 'Turn the Other Cheek'?" *Mental Health Matters*, episode 37, podcast. Available at https://saintlouiscounseling.org/mental-health-matters/ive-been-wronged-do-i-have-to-turn-the-other-cheek/.

Shan Kuo-hsi, Cardinal Paul, SJ. Holy See Press Office (August 23, 2012). Available at https://www.vatican.va/news_services/press/documentazione/documents/cardinali_biografie/cardinali_bio_shan-kuo-hsi_p_en.html.

Skrzyński, Henry. *The Jewess Mary, Mother of Jesus*. Kensington, Australia: Chevalier, 1994.